D1022103

Praise for *The End of Competitive Advantage*

"*The End of Competitive Advantage* is an incredibly practical playbook for competing in today's dynamic world. Rita McGrath's compelling book provides clear guidance for leaders searching for the competitive edges that seem to grow more elusive by the day. A must-read."

—Scott Anthony, Managing Partner, Innosight; author,
The Little Black Book of Innovation

"Rita Gunther McGrath cements her status as one of the top business gurus in the world with *The End of Competitive Advantage*. She asserts that sustainable competitive advantage is obsolete and offers a thoroughly compelling argument that successfully managing waves of transient advantage is the future of business success."

—John Caddell, author, *The Mistake Bank* (forthcoming)

"In today's economy, committing to achieve sustainable competitive advantage is like building the Maginot Line: It locks you into a position from which it is hard to move, and it does not keep the bad guys out. Better instead to adopt Rita McGrath's playbook for exploiting transient competitive advantages and get your organization to embrace the fact that the only constant is change."

—Geoffrey Moore, author, *Crossing the Chasm*
and *Escape Velocity*

"How do you strategize when sustainable competitive advantages are gone? You need a playbook for strategy that fits today's fast and uncertain world. You need new methods for organizing and acting to deliver continuous growth and profits over decades. You need a new competitive advantage—this book."

—Alex Osterwalder, entrepreneur and cofounder, Strategyzer.com

"McGrath's central insight is authentic, empirical, and profound. Too many organizations unicorn-hunt for 'sustainable' competitive advantage at the expense of investing in agile—and anticipatory—strategic opportunities. This book will provoke useful arguments around creating versus exploiting innovation opportunism."

—Michael Schrage, Research Fellow, MIT Sloan's Center for Digital Business; author, *Who Do You Want Your Customers to Become?*

"If competitive advantage was *ever* sustainable, that time has passed. McGrath's book not only captures the shortcomings of traditional, static models, but lays out the tools that fuel leading performance. *The End of Competitive Advantage* will give you an entirely new perspective on how to think about strategy."

—Francisco D'Souza, CEO, Cognizant

"This smart, readable book addresses today's most significant strategy reality: that we are living in an era of transient advantage. Rita McGrath provides a playbook for this new landscape, showing how you can identify opportunities fast, execute against them at scale, and be unafraid to move on when the situation changes."

—William D. Green, former Chairman, Accenture

"The urge to hold on to one's established competitive advantage is a vicious trap. McGrath clearly establishes the factors central to building a dynamic competitive edge for an enterprise of tomorrow. Refreshing, insightful, and a must-read."

—Sanjay Purohit, Senior Vice President, Infosys Ltd.

"McGrath's groundbreaking work is aptly timed for today's dynamic markets, where winning requires continuous reconfiguration."

—Nancy McKinstry, CEO and Chairman, Executive Board,
Wolters Kluwer nv

"*The End of Competitive Advantage* makes clear that high-performance teams have to stay vigilant. Are your leaders seizing new opportunities or just trying to optimize an outdated strategy? Keep your head up and stay alert, or a transient advantage might pass you by."

—Klaus C. Kleinfeld, Chairman and CEO, Alcoa

"As a long-time member of the Rita McGrath fan club, I was delighted to see this book. Her approach to strategy is fresh and practical, and is exactly what managers need today. It acknowledges competitive realities but shows a clear path forward. It is one of the most illuminating takes on how to deal with disruption that I have ever read."

—Clayton M. Christensen, Kim B. Clark Professor of Business
Administration, Harvard Business School

THE END OF COMPETITIVE ADVANTAGE

THE END OF COMPETITIVE ADVANTAGE

HOW TO KEEP YOUR STRATEGY MOVING AS FAST AS YOUR BUSINESS

Rita Gunther McGrath

Harvard Business Review Press

Boston, Massachusetts

The web addresses referenced in this book were live and correct at the time
of the book's publication but may be subject to change.

Library of Congress Cataloging-in-Publication Data

McGrath, Rita Gunther.
  The end of competitive advantage: how to keep your strategy moving as fast
  as your business/Rita McGrath.
      pages cm
  Includes bibliographical references.
  ISBN 978-1-4221-7281-0 (alk. paper)
  1. Strategic planning. 2. Competition. I. Title.
  HD30.28.M38378 2013
  658.4'012–dc23
                          2012051721

ISBN13: 9781422172810
eISBN: 9781422191415

You jolted me from complacency in my nice little bureaucratic job.

Said that if it were a "top five" school the PhD would be worth doing—otherwise not.

We started a family, left the city we both loved, moved away from our friends, and got a mortgage.

I was miserable. Transitions are hard.

But we went on to build something quite remarkable—together.

For John, and discovering what our next chapter holds.

Contents

Foreword

This book could not be more timely. Any leader seeking to understand what it takes to win in the ruthlessly competitive markets most of us are faced with today will benefit from reading it. In my thirty-two years as a retailer (beginning as a "Saturday boy" at Boots in Glasgow), I have personally witnessed a dramatic acceleration of the pace of change and the upending of assumptions we used to take for granted. Shopping behavior is changing dramatically. We are witnessing the end of advantages that made our 163-year-old Boots brand iconic. Consumers give businesses less permission to be wrong than ever before, and the Boots brand is not immune to this shift.

We were first introduced to Rita's ideas when Boots Group merged with Alliance UniChem in 2006 to form Alliance Boots, and the breathing room that followed allowed us to take this newly formed company private in 2007. At that time we decided to transform the organization in a way that would enable us to operate very differently—by putting our customers first. Working with Rita, who is a gifted and original strategic thinker, we sought to embed many of the principles presented in this book into the leadership mind-set of our new organization. And we continue to do that today. We seek to be quicker and more decisive. We seek to be more candid, so that pending news—even negative news—travels fast and is immediately addressed. We seek to spend more time thinking about the future than we ever have before. We seek to break down silos so that our organization is appropriately structured to capture opportunities and act as one unified entity. Most of all, we seek to create courageous leaders—leaders who regard the fast pace of competitive exchange as exciting and who are fully engaged in creating an organization that can boldly capture opportunities and just as boldly move away from strategies and business practices that no longer represent opportunities.

When we started our evolution, many observers were skeptical. The Boots brand was tired and undervalued, they said, and the strategy poorly explained and not all that well executed. Moreover, our new business model, which combined a business-to-business wholesale operation with a customer-focused retail business, had seldom proved to be successful. But our results have proven our critics wrong. Measures assessing the recognition of our brand, satisfaction of our customers, and engagement of our employees are at record levels, and the profitability of Alliance Boots has been increasing by at least 10 percent every year since its privatization. And all this was achieved despite the global recession.

Our evolution, like yours, is far from over. We believe, however, that the concept of strategy presented in this book is invaluable. Strategy needs to change because customers and markets are changing faster than ever. The ideas in these pages provide a much-needed guide to a world of transient competitive advantage.

—Alex Gourlay
   Chief Executive, Health & Beauty Division, Alliance Boots
   Nottingham, United Kingdom, January 2013

Preface

Strategy is stuck. If you dropped into a boardroom discussion or an executive team meeting, chances are you'd hear a lot of strategic thinking based on ideas and frameworks designed in, and for, a different era. The biggies—such as Michael Porter's five forces analysis, BCG's growth-share matrix for analyzing corporate portfolios, and Hamel and Prahalad's core competence of the firm—are all tremendously important ideas.[1] Many strategies today are still informed by them. But virtually all strategy frameworks and tools + in use today are based on a single dominant idea: that the purpose of strategy is to achieve a sustainable competitive advantage. This idea is strategy's most fundamental concept. It's every company's holy grail. And it's no longer relevant for more and more companies.

In this book, I take on the idea of sustainable competitive advantage and argue that executives need to stop basing their strategies on it. In its place, I offer a perspective on strategy that is based on the idea of transient competitive advantage: that to win in volatile and uncertain environments, executives need to learn how to exploit short-lived opportunities with speed and decisiveness. I argue that the deeply ingrained structures and systems that executives rely on to extract maximum value from a competitive advantage are liabilities—outdated and even dangerous—in a fast-moving competitive environment.

This much at least seems to be well understood. But then why hasn't basic strategy practice changed? Most executives, even when they realize that competitive advantages are going to be ephemeral, are still using strategy frameworks and tools designed for achieving a sustainable competitive advantage, not for quickly exploiting and moving in and out of advantages.

This book addresses that problem. It offers a new set of practices based on the notion of transient, not sustainable, competitive advantage. With this book, you'll get a new playbook for strategy—one that is based on a new set of assumptions about how the world works—and learn how some of the most successful companies in the world use the new playbook to compete and win when competitive advantages are transient.

The Evolution of Strategy

How did the idea of sustainable competitive advantage get so entrenched in the first place? Let me retrace how this concept evolved and, in parallel, show how my own work—both in academia and in the world of management practice—has led up to this book.

Sustainable Competitive Advantage

Historically, strategy and innovation have been thought of as two separate disciplines, in both research and practice. Strategy was all about finding a favorable position in a well-defined industry and then exploiting a long-term competitive advantage. Innovation was about creating new businesses and was seen as something separate from the business's core set of activities. Initially, I studied the corporate innovation process, much of which is laid out in my previous coauthored books.[2] At the time, relatively few serious scholars were studying "corporate venturing," with a few exceptions such as Bob Burgelman; Kathy Eisenhardt; and, of course, my coauthor, mentor, and colleague Ian C. MacMillan.[3] Instead, most of my PhD colleagues were busy studying positional dynamics within industries (with the goal of understanding how to achieve sustainable competitive advantages).

My academic work at that time had mostly to do with fostering entrepreneurial behavior within large firms. A major insight from those days was that when you're trying to enter fields in which you don't have a broad-based platform of experience—in other words, areas in which the ratio of assumptions you have to make relative to knowledge that you possess is high—a different set of disciplines needs to be employed. Ian MacMillan and I wrote a suggested approach to tackling this dilemma in "Discovery-Driven Planning," a best-selling article in *Harvard Business Review* that has since become a staple of entrepreneurship and innovation courses.[4] We didn't realize it at the time, but we were laying the foundations for a new approach to strategy, in which sustainable competitive advantage wasn't really the point.

The Growing Gap between Traditional Approaches to Strategy and the Real World

I had the opportunity to apply many of these ideas with consulting clients as we sought to help them develop an innovation proficiency. But this is when it started becoming obvious to us that most companies we were working with were really having trouble with their basic strategy for competing in their core businesses. Diverse clients such as DuPont, 3M, Nokia, Intel, and IBM were all beginning to recognize that traditional approaches to strategy and innovation weren't keeping pace with the speed of the markets in which they were competing.

But even as management tools to supposedly help cope with the pace of competition proliferated, executives didn't use them. Executives reported to the consultancy Bain "that the speed of the new economy has caused people and firms to believe they don't have time to implement tools," and firms, particularly in North America, were feeling "understaffed," with the consequence that they were sticking increasingly to tools they had already had experience with. Ironically, at the time, despite a lot of innovation in management tools and approaches, firms were increasing their reliance on strategy tools that they had inherited from the past.[5] So although they talked about using increasingly sophisticated approaches, if you looked at what they were really working with you would still find SWOT analyses, industry analyses, and rather conventional competitive analysis.[6] Although executives realized the need for new approaches to strategy, they were still using old ones—or none at all.

Along with this growing gap in practice, some scholars in academia started to question the idea of sustainable competitive advantage. Ian MacMillan was one of the first to tease out its specific implications for strategy. Competitive advantage, he reasoned, could best be thought of in waves, with the job of the strategist being to seize strategic initiative by launching ever-new waves.[7] He and Rich D'Aveni coined the term "hypercompetition" to characterize markets in which a firm's competitive advantage would be quickly competed away.[8]

In both business and academia there was an increasing sense that existing frameworks were not doing a great job helping leaders cope with the faster pace of competition. And then, with the advent of the internet and the knowledge-based economy in general, decreases in protective trade regulations, and technological advances, things seemed to move ever faster, and for some reason companies that you would think would be able to cope lost their edge. Max Boisot, a dear and now departed friend, summed up the implications for unstable advantage in knowledge-intensive industries, basically concluding that the most profitable point in the evolution of an advantage was also its most fragile.[9] By the late 1990s, the connection between innovation and strategy went mainstream with the publication of Clay Christensen's *The Innovator's Dilemma*,[10] which cited discovery-driven planning as a useful element of the strategists' toolkit while trying to do innovative things.[11]

Transient Competitive Advantage

What was starting to happen was that the disparate fields of competitive strategy, innovation, and organizational change were all coming together. This in turn meant we needed to add new frameworks and tools for practicing strategy to the well-entrenched ones such as five forces analysis and the growth-share matrix. In my previous books, *Harvard Business Review* and journal articles, talks, and consulting, I've tried over the years to sketch out what a new way of practicing strategy might look like. Options reasoning, for instance, is a way of making investments in the future without having to risk massive losses.[12] Intelligent failures can be helpful in facilitating learning.[13] Opportunity recognition is a skill that can be enhanced and developed in a systematic way.[14] The resource allocation process is perhaps the most significant way to influence what gets done in an organization and who does it.[15] You need to think of customer "jobs to be done," rather than rigid markets influenced by supply and demand.[16] Business model innovation was every bit as important as R&D or product innovation.[17] And different leadership behaviors need to be deployed in businesses with different levels of maturity.[18]

The implications of all these ideas came together in what I'm calling in this book a new playbook for strategy. The new playbook is based on a new set of assumptions about how the world works—a different set of assumptions from those that gave us the useful frameworks and tools we've been using for the past several decades. The strategy playbook today needs to be based on the idea of transient competitive advantage—that is, where you compete, how you compete, and how you win is very different when competitive advantage is no longer sustainable.

Basing your strategies on a new set of assumptions can seem daunting, even if you know it's the right thing to do. Even more challenging is shifting the ultimate goal of your strategy from a sustainable competitive advantage to a transient one—you can no longer plan to squeeze as much as you can out of any existing competitive advantage unless you are already well into exploring a new one. But as you'll see from the stories in this book from companies and leaders all over the world who are competing on transient advantages, once you start working with the new strategic playbook, changes in the configuration of your advantages don't have to be intimidating at all. Some of the executives I interviewed actually seemed to be having fun—rather than being defensive and debilitated, they used the pursuit of transient competitive advantages to represent a compelling and engaging call to action for their people and a spur to innovation.

Fast-moving strategies have implications for managerial careers as well. A friend of mine working for a Brazilian company suggested a somewhat counterintuitive idea: "In Brazil," he said, "we've been through it all—inflation, corruption, unpredictable governmental regulation, you name it. And you know, you get good at it." He pointed out that managers whose only experience is with more tame types of competition would be flummoxed if they had to confront some of the challenges his generation of leaders in Brazil had to overcome on a routine basis.

Although it's easy to see the devastation wreaked on companies whose leaders were not prepared to be dynamically competitive, I think it's important to recognize the benefits, too. Sclerotic and inefficient industries get better when faced with genuine competitive threats. Would anyone want to go back to the days in which the government-owned telephone company dictated pricing and choices, for instance? In their quest to find the next opportunity, companies are getting better at figuring out what people really need and will pay for, at designing better experiences, and at wresting new efficiencies from existing assets. In a lot of cases, the value an average person gets for the same dollar, yen, or euro is vastly greater than it was even a decade or two ago. And there are more opportunities for new ideas and for young companies to thrive than ever before.

Before closing this preface, I'd like to acknowledge some of the people who have been instrumental in making this book a reality. Jill S. Dailey, of Accenture, proved invaluable as an intellectual sparring partner, a source of new ideas, and a resource for figuring out how these ideas could work in practice. The idea of arenas and of industries competing with industries is an idea we've worked on pretty intensively together. Ian MacMillan was a sounding board and an unapologetic critic of those ideas he didn't feel made sense. I appreciated the suggestions and comments of the many people I interviewed for the book. Alison Norman, Xi Zhang, and Sooreen Lee provided invaluable research assistance. Melinda Merino and the team at Harvard Business Review Press have been true partners in crafting and shaping the ideas presented here.

I hope you enjoy this introduction to people and companies that I believe represent some of the best new strategic thinking and behavior for winning even when competitive advantages don't last. They don't always get it right—in fact, if my ideas about temporary advantage and learning from failure apply, it's almost impossible for a company to call it correctly every time. What matters, though, when you have been taken by surprise or something negative occurs, is what you do next. The best firms look candidly at what happened, figure out how to do it better the next time, and move on. It's a bit like surfing a wave—you might fall off and find yourself embarrassedly paddling back to shore, but great surfers get back on that board. So too with great companies. They move from wave to wave of competitive advantages, trying not to stay with one too long because it will become exhausted, and always looking for the next one. It has been fun getting to know them.

—Rita Gunther McGrath
Princeton Junction, New Jersey

THE END OF
COMPETITIVE
ADVANTAGE

1

The End of Competitive Advantage

Fuji Photo Film Company had an inauspicious beginning. It was divested from Japan's first cinematic film manufacturer in the 1930s because it was a chronic underperformer. Over the years, it improved its poor reputation for quality, became a significant global firm, and began to take on giants such as Eastman Kodak in film and film processing. The market for amateur and professional chemical-based photographic processes hadn't really changed in over a hundred years, meaning that competition tended to devolve around distribution rather than products, and Fuji struggled to break into markets in which Kodak was entrenched. There were many innovations, to be sure—including roll film, 35-millimeter film, easy-to-load cartridges, and even disposable cameras—but the basic position of film at the center of the photography industry's competitive universe hadn't changed for decades.

In the 1970s, however, an event that subsequently proved seminal to the evolution of the photography business took place. Two members of one of America's wealthiest families, Nelson Bunker Hunt and William Herbert Hunt, made a play to corner the silver market. They were interested in using silver as a hedge against inflation (a big issue at the time) and also as a diversifying asset class given that they had large holdings in oil. They began to make investments in silver in 1973, at which point the price of an ounce of silver was just under $2. In early 1979, the price had risen to about $5. By the time their plans were publicly exposed at the end of 1979, they had amassed more than 100 million ounces (6.25 million pounds) of silver, which observers guessed was about half the world's supply. Their actions caused the price of silver to jump to a mind-boggling number of over $50 per ounce.[1]

The consternation among manufacturers was palpable—what would happen if silver, a key ingredient in film processing, proved far more expensive than their economic models had predicted? Further, what if the investors in silver had such a lock on the market that there would not be enough of the material to go around? Their anxiety didn't last long, however, because in March of 1980 the price of silver collapsed precipitously, bringing with it collateral damage in the form of one of the sharpest declines in the Dow Jones Industrial Average ever experienced.[2] With the crisis over, most photography companies, Kodak among them, settled back into doing business as usual.

Minoru Ohnishi, who became CEO of Fuji Photo Film in 1980, remained deeply uneasy about the experience, however. He sensed that a fundamental change was potentially afoot in the photography business. The introduction of Sony's first digital camera, the Mavica, in 1984 created the reality of photography that could do without film. He said later, "That's when I realized film-less technology was possible."[3] He wasted no time moving on this insight. He invested heavily in building up expertise in digital technologies to prepare for the next round of competition in the photography business. His determination for the company to make this transition was described as "single-minded" by a writer for *BusinessWeek*, who observed that if one were to tally up Fuji's investments by 1999 in research and technology dedicated to digital products, it would easily top $2 billion. The article went on to note a "mystical" belief among the company employees in the correctness of this strategy. This attitude was reflected by chief scientist and senior advisor Hirozo Ueda, who told the reporter, "We're not going to quit, and we're not going to lose this battle."[4] By 2003, Fujifilm had nearly five thousand digital processing labs in chain stores throughout the United States; at the time, Kodak had less than a hundred.[5]

Ohnishi was determined not only to keep his company relevant in digital technologies for photography, but also to extend its reach to opportunities outside the photography business. He pushed the company to establish a sales channel for new products such as magnetic tape optics and hybrid electronic systems. It became the first non-US company to produce videotape. Later diversification efforts took the firm into biotechnology and office automation. It entered floppy disk manufacturing. Ohnishi was an innovator in business processes at Fuji as well. In a Japanese context famous for its long-tenured "salarymen," Ohnishi championed a lean head-quarters staff, even going to great lengths to benchmark how well Fuji compared with forty other Japanese companies with respect to how many staff were involved in overhead functions. Although Fuji came in at 9 percent (and the average of the rest was 16.7 percent), Ohnishi was determined to bring this ratio down to 7 percent by asking the organization to cut its workload significantly and to eliminate 50 percent of the time-consuming consensus building and documentation that were standard business practice at the time.[6]

The reconfiguration of the company continued after Ohnishi was replaced by Shigetaka Komori, with sometimes-painful transitions as jobs were lost and facilities closed. The firm aggressively pulled resources from the photographic film business, reportedly cutting more than $2.5 billion in costs in order to invest those resources in new businesses.[7] Today, Fujifilm has significant health care and electronics operations and obtains some 45 percent of its revenue from document solutions and office printers.[8] All this was accomplished during several decades in which Japan's domestic industries were moribund and the country seemed unable to escape stagnation. In 2011, Fujifilm generated $25 billion in revenue, employed more than 78,000 people, and ranked 377th on *Fortune*'s Global 500 list. Kodak has gone bankrupt.

Fuji's story suggests that simply managing well, developing quality products, and building up well-recognized brands is insufficient to remain on top in increasingly heated global competition. The stakes for the company were huge—it risked undermining its existing advantages, and had to make a bet on a highly uncertain future. Yet, ultimately, it was Fuji's approach—investing in new advantages and pulling resources from declining ones—that proved to be more robust in the face of change. It didn't get it right every time, and sometimes the transitions were painful. But the company didn't get trapped by its past.

When competitive advantages don't last, or last for a much shorter time than they used to, the strategy playbook needs to change. Leaders have inherited a lot of ideas that may have made sense at one point but aren't keeping up with the pace of strategic change today. Although executives realize that rapid change is the norm, the strategies they use to compete still draw on frameworks and practices that were most effective decades ago. Executives need a new set of strategy frameworks and practices for winning over the long haul, even as sustainable competitive advantages have become a thing of the past.

This book is about the dynamics of transient, rather than sustainable, competitive advantage. It shows the new strategic logic—where to compete, how to compete, and how to win—when competitive advantages are temporary, and shows what we can learn from companies that have learned to ride the wave from one transient advantage to another.

Your Strategy Is Based on Old Assumptions

Sony. Research In Motion (RIM). Blockbuster. Circuit City. Even the New York Stock Exchange. The list of once-storied organizations that are either gone or are no longer relevant is a long one. Their downfall is a predictable outcome of practices that are designed around the concept of sustainable competitive advantage. The fundamental problem is that deeply ingrained structures and systems designed to extract maximum value from a competitive advantage become a liability when the environment requires instead the capacity to surf through waves of short-lived opportunities. To compete in these more volatile and uncertain environments, you need to do things differently.

When I got my start in the strategy field, there were two foundational assumptions we took practically as gospel. The first was that *industry matters most*. We were taught that industries consist of relatively enduring and stable competitive forces—take the time and effort to deeply understand these forces, and voilà, you can create a road map for your other decisions that is likely to last for some time. The emphasis in strategy was therefore analytical: because industries were assumed to be relatively stable, you could get a decent payoff by investing in analytical capabilities to spot industry trends and design your strategy accordingly. Those were the days of the five-year plan. A major assumption was that the world of five years from now was to some extent comprehensible today.

For instance, the traditional network television model in the United States was successful for many decades because the limited and expensive broadcast spectrum meant that a few players (in this case the major networks) dominated the few channels to customers. Constraints having to do with geography, syndication rights, and ratings all kept the model in place for years. For advertisers, this meant that television stations offered the promise of extremely large mass markets. Over the last thirty years, the constraints that held this model in place have eroded. Cable television eliminated the constraint of limited channels, fragmenting the mass market. Video rentals allowed viewers to watch content at their own convenience. The ability to record programs and skip the commercials was later embraced by a public weary of intrusive advertisements. More recently, the internet has facilitated an explosion of "channels" that viewers might look to for entertainment. This relaxation of constraints has fundamentally undermined the networks' business model. Indeed, the most important dynamic wasn't network-to-network competition but an invasion from other industries.

The second assumption was that *once achieved, advantages are sustainable*. Having achieved a solid position within an industry, companies were encouraged to optimize their people, assets, and systems around these advantages. In a world of lasting advantage, it made sense to promote people who were good at running big businesses, operated with greater efficiency, wrung costs out of the system, and otherwise preserved the advantage. Management structures that directed resources and talent to strong core businesses, often called "strategic business units," were associated with high performance. The core assumption here was that you could optimize your systems and processes around a set of sustainable advantages.

There are indeed examples of advantages that can be sustained, even today. Capitalizing on deep customer relationships, making highly complicated machines such as airplanes, running a mine, and selling daily necessities such as food are all situations in which some companies have been able to exploit an advantage for some time. But in more and more sectors, and for more and more businesses, this is not what the world looks like any more. Music, high technology, travel, communication, consumer electronics, the automobile business, and even education are facing situations in which advantages are copied quickly, technology changes, or customers seek other alternatives and things move on.

The New Logic of Strategy

The assumption of sustainable advantage creates a bias toward stability that can be deadly. My research suggests that rather than stability being the normal state of things and change being the abnormal thing, it is actually the other way around. Stability, not change, is the state that is most dangerous in highly dynamic competitive environments.

Think about it: the presumption of stability creates all the wrong reflexes. It allows for inertia and power to build up along the lines of an existing business model. It allows people to fall into routines and habits of mind. It creates the conditions for turf wars and organizational rigidity. It inhibits innovation. It tends to foster the denial reaction rather than proactive design of a strategic next step. And yet "change management" is seen as an other-than-normal activity, requiring special attention, training, and resources. A Google search on the phrase "change management" turns up 21,600,000 results—that's twenty-one *million* citations.

A preference for equilibrium and stability means that many shifts in the marketplace are met by business leaders denying that these shifts mean anything negative for them. Consider the reaction of executives from Research In Motion (the parent company of BlackBerry devices) to the 2007 introduction of the iPhone. Jim Balsillie, the company's co-CEO, told a Reuters reporter that the launch of Apple's iPhone wasn't a major threat, simply the entry of yet another competitor into the smartphone market.[9] Five years later, the company is at risk for its very survival, facing a slew of disappointing product launches, subscriber defection, continuing service outages, and shareholders in open revolt. Its former leaders have been replaced. Yet this company's products were so beloved by its corporate users that asking them to put away their BlackBerries was like asking them to amputate a limb. What happened? A long track record of relatively stable success caused the ambition to hungrily search for new opportunities to atrophy. Once that's gone, it's hard to regain quickly in the face of fast competitive onslaughts.

It's typical for leaders to deny there is an issue until far too late, at which point there is an "all hands on deck" full-blown crisis. As one of my interview respondents from a major medical device manufacturer observed, "We had seen it coming, and decided to ignore it and put our fingers into our ears until it became so obvious that we could no longer ignore it." Only then are resources mobilized, teams formed, and a sense of urgency created. Unfortunately, by that time it is often too late. Strategy today instead needs to be based on a new set of assumptions and practices.

Where to Compete: Arenas, Not Industries

One of the biggest changes we need to make in our assumptions is that within-industry competition is the most significant competitive threat. Companies define their most important competitors as other companies within the same industry, meaning those firms offering products that are a close substitute for one another. This is a rather dangerous way to think about competition. In more and more markets, we are seeing industries competing with other industries, business models competing with business models even in the same industry, and entirely new categories emerging out of whole cloth. This is most obvious in those markets that have embraced the digital revolution—just look at the shrinking CD section of your local bookstore (if, of course, your local bookstore is still around) and you'll see what I mean. Indeed, a reporter for the *Wall Street Journal* recently observed that if you look at categories of purchases for the average American family, vehicle purchases, apparel and services, entertainment, and food away from home are all shrinking, some at double-digit rates. What's growing? Spending on telephone services, up by 11 percent since the 2007 introduction of the iPhone.[10]

It isn't that industries have stopped being relevant; it's just that using industry as a level of analysis is often not fine-grained enough to determine what is really going on at the level at which decisions need to be made. A new level of analysis that reflects the connection between market segment, offer, and geographic location at a granular level is needed. I call this an *arena*. Arenas are characterized by particular connections between customers and solutions, not by the conventional description of offerings that are near substitutes for one another.

To use a military analogy, battles are fought in particular geographic locations, with particular equipment, to beat particular rivals. Increasingly, business strategies need to be formulated with that level of precision. The driver of categorization will in all likelihood be the outcomes that particular customers seek ("jobs to be done") and the alternative ways those outcomes might be met. This is vital, because the most substantial threats to a given advantage are likely to arise from a peripheral or nonobvious location.

This further raises the issue that a firm may not have a single approach that holds for all the arenas in which it participates. Instead, the approach may be adapted to the particular arena and competitors it is facing. For example, consider the strategy of language-teaching firm Berlitz. As Marcos Justus, their former Brazilian president, told me, in Brazil, competition for the mass market was fierce, but competition for customers in the upper income brackets was less so. There, a strategy of focusing on the upper echelons and positioning the brand as an elite product made sense. In the United States, where the majority of customers are somewhere in the middle, a different positioning featuring convenience and flexibility made sense. These are two different strategies, responding to the exigencies of the two different arenas. Both of these strategies, however, drive Berlitz's evolution toward the cultural consultancy it aspires to become.

The arena concept also suggests that conventional ideas about what creates a long-lived advantage will change. Product features, new technologies, and the "better mousetrap" sorts of sources of advantage are proving to be less durable than we once thought. Instead, companies are learning to leverage more ephemeral things such as deep customer relationships and the ability to design irreplaceable experiences across multiple arenas. They will be focused on creating capabilities and skills that will be relevant to whatever arenas they happen to find themselves operating in. And they may even be more relaxed about traditional protections and barriers to entry, because competition will devolve around highly intangible and emotional factors.

There is a big difference between thinking about strategy in terms of arenas as opposed to industries. In industry analysis, the goal is often to determine one's relative position with respect to other players in the same industry. It's good to have a large market share. And competitive threats are of the traditional kind—moves regarding product introductions, pricing, promotions, and so on. It's very easy to be blindsided. In the 1980s, for instance, no money-center bank even saw the threat of Merrill Lynch's cash management account offering because it wasn't offered by a bank; millions in deposits flew out the door before anybody realized what was going on. More recently, Google's moves into telephone operating systems and online video have created consternation in traditional phone businesses; retailers such as Walmart are edging into health care; and the entire activity of making payments is being contested by players from a bunch of different industries, including mobile phone operators, internet credit providers, swipe card makers, and, of course, traditional credit and debit card providers.

Although this is oversimplifying things a bit, you can think of traditional strategic analysis as being somewhat like the game of chess, which is quite sophisticated and nuanced but in which the goal is to achieve a powerful competitive advantage in a major market, akin to checkmating one's opponent. Arena-based strategy is much more akin to the Japanese game of Go, in which the goal is to capture as much territory as possible—the winner in Go lays the strategic groundwork by adroit placement of pieces on a board, eventually capturing enough territory to overwhelm one's opponent.

The imagery of arena-based strategy is more that of orchestration than of plotting a compelling victory, and implementation on the ground by those actually confronting conditions within a specific arena becomes increasingly important (table 1-1).

TABLE 1-1

Where to compete: industry perspective versus arena perspective

	Industry	Arena
Goal	Positional advantage	Capturing territory
Measure of success	Market share	Share of potential opportunity spaces
Biggest threat	Intraindustry competitive moves	Interindustry moves; disruption of existing model
Definition of customer segment	Demographic or geographic	Behavioral
Key drivers	Comparative price, functionality, quality	"Jobs to be done" in total customer experience
Likely acquisition behavior	Within-industry consolidation or beyond-industry diversification	Bolt-on for new capability acquisition, often across industry boundaries
Metaphor	Chess	Japanese game of Go

How to Compete: Temporary, Not Sustainable, Competitive Advantage

You can think of the evolution of a particular competitive advantage in several phases, as illustrated in figure 1-1. During the launch process, a firm organizes to grasp a new opportunity. During launch, opportunities are identified, resources allocated, and a team is assembled to create something new. This is where innovation comes in.

If the opportunity gets traction, the advantage begins to enjoy a period of ramping up: from the initial few segments, more and more are captured, and the business gains ground. Systems and processes to get the business to scale are implemented. Experiments become full-scale market introductions. Speed is often critical here: ramp up too slowly, and competitors can quickly match what you are doing and destroy your differentiation.

After a successful ramp-up, the company can enjoy a period—sometimes quite a long period—of exploitation, in which the

FIGURE 1-1

How to compete: the wave of transient advantage

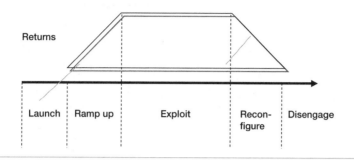

business is operating well and generating reasonable profits. During the exploitation phase of a transient advantage, a firm has established a clear point of differentiation from competitors in a way that its customers appreciate and is enjoying the benefits. During exploitation, market share growth and profitability typically expand, more and more customers are adopting, prices and margins are attractive, and competitors see your organization as the one to beat. The goal is to understand how this period can be extended for as long as possible while simultaneously being mindful that it will eventually erode.

Managing the exploitation phase well means focusing on those few key areas in which a firm has achieved meaningful competitive separation. Within those spaces, managers need to manage competitive moves and countermoves, build highly scalable competencies for the next innovation, make sure that new advantages are eventually integrated into the firm's core offerings as a legitimate part of the company, and remain alert to threats and opportunities from different areas. One really wants to prevent excessive build-up of assets and people during the exploitation phase, because these will create barriers to moving on to the next advantage. Even as the existing advantages are generating good results, leaders need to be pulling assets and resources out of them to create resource space for the next advantage, just as Fuji did with its film-based photography business.

With temporary advantages, the existing model will always come under pressure, suggesting the need for reconfiguration and renewal of the advantage (in essence, launching a new wave). The reconfiguration process is central to succeeding in transient-advantage situations, because it is through reconfiguration that assets, people, and capabilities make the transition from one advantage to another. During reconfiguration, teams that might have been engaged to ramp up or exploit an advantage are shifted to some other set of activities, assets are changed or redeployed, and people move from one assignment to the next. Rather than viewing such reorganizations as negative, as they often are in a sustainable-advantage context, they are taken for granted as necessary and useful in a transient-advantage world. Indeed, not having such dynamism in the structures and processes in place in an organization can be seen as negative by the employees.

Finally, when an advantage is exhausted, the opportunity undergoes a process of erosion, suggesting the need for disengagement. Through the disengagement process, a firm disposes of the assets and other capabilities that are no longer relevant to its future, either by selling them, shutting them down, or repurposing them. The objective is to manage this process gracefully and quickly. Long, drawn-out disengagements do little more than consume resources without making the end result any more pleasant. In a transient-advantage context, unlike a conventional one, disengaging is not confused with business failure. Indeed, disengagement can and should take place when a business is still viable, rather than when a desperate organization has no other choice.

In many organizations, the center of gravity is determined so much by the businesses in "exploit" mode that the other parts of this process are neglected. That matters, because different disciplines and skills sets are useful in different parts of this wave. The launch and ramp-up processes require innovators and experiment-ers who are comfortable with ambiguity and prepared to learn. The exploitation phase needs people who thrive on designing effective processes and making things systematic. The disengagement phase requires those who are good at seeing early evidence of decline and unafraid to make the sometimes-difficult decisions to stop doing something.

In an organization of any complexity, part of the challenge from the strategists' point of view is that you will have many such waves playing out, in different phases, all at the same time. The job of orchestrating how these waves are managed is increasingly a crucial part of the CEO's challenge. That is what this book is about.

How to Win: Companies That Manage the Wave of Transient Advantage Well

As part of the research for this book, I set out to find companies that have figured out how to cope, even to thrive, amidst the challenge of moving from one advantage to the next for a reasonably long period of time.

In 2010, my research team tracked down every publicly traded company on any global exchange with a market capitalization of over $1 billion US dollars as of the end of 2009 (4,793 firms). Then we examined how many of these firms had been able to grow revenue or net income by at least 5 percent every year for the preceding five years (in other words, from 2004 to 2009). Note that what we were inter-ested in here was not total returns or compound annual growth, but rather steady annual growth, year in, year out. The reason we picked 5 percent was that global gross domestic product (GDP) growth hovered around 4 percent during this time period, and our thinking was that truly outstanding companies should be able to exceed this level.[11] The results were surprising. Only 8 percent of the firms were above the revenue growth threshold of 5 percent every year, and only 4 percent of the firms were above the net income threshold.

"Well," we thought, "perhaps we're not being fair—after all, the Great Recession that began in 2008 may have knocked normally well-managed firms for a loop." So we redid the study, but this time from 2000 to 2004. The numbers were a little better, but not hugely so: 15 percent and 7 percent for revenue and net income, respectively. Now, however, we were intrigued—companies that managed to grow consistently were evidently far from average. We then took the entire ten-year period (from 2000 to 2009) and examined how many firms were able to deliver steady-as-you-go growth. Exactly ten managed to grow net income consistently by at least 5 percent during the study period.

The companies that grew net income consistently were Cognizant Technology Solutions (United States), HDFC Bank (India), FactSet (United States), ACS (Spain), Krka (Slovenia), Infosys (India), Tsingtao Brewery (China), Yahoo! Japan (Japan), Atmos Energy (United States), and Indra Sistemas (Spain). I call this group of extremely unusual firms (0.25 percent of the total) *growth outliers* because their steady performance, even in the face of massive change and uncertainty, was so unusual (table 1-2).

I took each firm and compared it first with its top three competitors (as indicated by Hoover's Business Research) and then with each other to glean insights about what allowed these firms to achieve such consistent, steady growth. The major conclusion was that this group of firms was pursuing strategies with a long-term perspective on where they wanted to go, but also with the recognition that whatever they were doing today wasn't going to drive their future growth. Interestingly, they had identified and implemented ways of combining tremendous internal stability while motivating tremendous external agility, particularly in terms of business models. We will learn more from them—and other companies that seem to have embraced operating in this new environment—as the book unfolds. They are

TABLE 1-2

How to win: the growth outliers

Outlier company	Original country	What it does
Cognizant Technology Solutions	United States	Founded in 1994 as Dun & Bradstreet's technology services arm and spun off two years later. Began with primarily application maintenance work. Originally a "tactical source of inexpensive talent," according to the company website.
HDFC Bank	India	Founded in 1994 with the dream of becoming a world-class private Indian bank.
FactSet	United States	Founded in 1978 to automate the creation of financial analysis reports for analysts and companies (not individual investors). Began with a short paper report on companies, circulated to a few key clients, called "Company Factset."
ACS	Spain	ACS is a Spanish construction and services provider formed from the merger and revitalization of formerly struggling, separate companies.
Krka	Slovenia	Founded in 1954, Krka is a Slovenian pharmaceutical manufacturer expanding from its base to neighboring regional markets.
Infosys	India	Founded by six engineers in India in 1981, Infosys began as an India-based information technology services provider with one client.
Tsingtao Brewery	China	The Tsingtao Brewery was founded in 1903 by German settlers in Qingdao, China.
Yahoo! Japan	Japan	US–based Yahoo! and Tokyo-based Softbank set up internet portal Yahoo! Japan in 1996 as a joint venture. It is an independent, publicly listed company.
Atmos Energy	United States	Atmos Energy is the largest gas-only utility in the United States. It has both a regulated arm, which distributes natural gas, and a nonregulated subsidiary, Atmos Energy Services.
Indra Sistemas	Spain	Indra Sistemas is a diversified global technology company that operates in a wide range of sectors, including transport and traffic, energy and industry, public administration and health care, financial services, security and defense, and telecommunications and media.

operating with a new playbook for strategy—a playbook based on new assumptions of competing in arenas (not industries alone) and exploiting temporary competitive advantages, not sustainable ones.

The New Strategy Playbook

The end of competitive advantage means that the assumptions that underpin much of what we used to believe about running organizations are deeply flawed. The rest of this book will explore what that means for business leaders and how the world will look different (table 1-3). Some of the new playbook is well understood already, such as the need to pursue innovation (although firms still struggle to get it right in practice). Other elements of the new playbook have received little emphasis in conversations about strategy, such as the practice of continuous reconfiguration and disengagement. I'll take up those topics first in the discussion that follows, and then spend some time on the more general challenges of the new strategy playbook.

"Continuous Reconfiguration" (chapter 2) explores how companies can build the capability to move from arena to arena, rather than trying to defend existing competitive advantages. Companies that can do this show a remarkable degree of both stability and dynamism. Moving from advantage to advantage is seen as quite normal, not exceptional. Clinging to older advantages is seen as potentially dangerous. Exits are seen as intelligent, and failures as potential harbingers of useful insight. Most important, companies develop a rhythm for moving from arena to arena, with each one being managed as its particular life cycle stage suggests. And rather than the wrenching downsizings and restructurings that are so common in business today, disengagements occur in a steady rhythm, rather than in high dramas.

TABLE 1-3

The new strategy playbook

	From	To
Continuous reconfiguration (chapter 2)	Extreme downsizing or restructuring	Continuous morphing
	Emphasis on exploitation phase	Equal emphasis on entire wave
	Stability or dynamism alone	Stability combined with dynamism
	Narrowly defined jobs and roles	Fluidity in allocation of talent
	Stable vision, monolithic execution	Stable vision, variety in execution
Healthy disengagement (chapter 3)	Defending an advantage to the bitter end	Ending advantages frequently, formally, and systematically
	Exit viewed as strategically undesirable	Emphasis on retaining learning from exits
	Exits occur unexpectedly and with great drama	Exits occur in a steady rhythm
	Focus only on objective facts	Focus on subjective early warnings
Using resource allocation to promote deftness (chapter 4)	Resources held hostage in business units	Key resources under central control
	Squeezing opportunities into the existing structure	Organizing around opportunities
	Attempts to extend the useful life of assets for as long as possible	Aggressive and proactive retirement of competitively obsolete assets
	Terminal value	Asset debt
	Capital budgeting mind-set	Real options mind-set
	Investment-intensive strategic initiatives	Parsimony, parsimony, parsimony
	Ownership is key	Access is key
	Build it yourself	Leverage external resources
Building an innovation proficiency (chapter 5)	Innovation is episodic	Innovation is an ongoing, systematic process
	Governance and budgeting done the same way across the business	Governance and budgeting for innovation separate from business as usual

(continued)

The new strategy playbook (continued)

	Resources devoted primarily to exploitation	A balanced portfolio of initiatives that support the core, build new platforms, and invest in options
	People work on innovation in addition to their day jobs	Resources dedicated to innovation activities
	Failure to test assumptions; relatively little learning	Assumptions continually tested; learning informs major business decisions
	Failures avoided and not discussable	Intelligent failures encouraged
	Planning orientation	Experimental orientation
	Begin with our offerings and innovate to extend them to new areas	Begin with customers and innovate to help them get their jobs done
Leadership and mind-set (chapter 6)	Assumption that existing advantages will persist	Assumption that existing advantages will come under pressure
	Conversations that reinforce existing perspectives	Conversations that candidly question the status quo
	Relatively few and homogenous people involved in strategy process	Broader constituencies involved in strategy process, with diverse inputs
	Precise but slow	Fast and roughly right
	Prediction oriented	Discovery driven
	Net present value oriented	Options oriented
	Seeking confirmation	Seeking disconfirmation
	Talent directed to solving problems	Talent directed to identifying and seizing opportunities
	Extending a trajectory	Promoting continual shifts
	Accepting a failing trajectory	Picking oneself up quickly
Personal meaning of transient advantage (chapter 7)	Emphasis on analytical strategizing	Emphasis on rapid execution
	Organizational systems	Individual skills
	A stable career path	A series of gigs
	Hierarchies and teams	Individual superstars
	Infrequent job hunting	Permanent career campaigns
	Careers managed by the organization	Careers managed by the individual

As Sanjay Purohit, the head of planning for Infosys, recounted at a recent Columbia executive education course at which he was a guest speaker, about every two to three years the company reorganizes. By doing this, it breaks up a lot of the inertia and complexity that grow in any organization over time. In addition, it continuously moves people out of projects and activities that do not meet its threshold for continuously adding value into higher-value-added activities. Infosys is quite disciplined about its selection of customers, refusing to serve those who do not help the company to develop new sources of value. Some might question the disorganization and cost of so much reorganizing, to which Sanjay replies, "The cost of reorganizing the company is nothing compared to the growth potential it unleashes. We work out what our new axis of growth will be, then reorganize the company to deliver to these axes."

One of the most significant differences between the assumption of sustainable competitive advantage and more dynamic strategy is that disengagement—the process of moving out of an exhausted opportunity—is as core to the business as innovation, growth, and exploitation are. Particular arenas are evaluated for withdrawal regularly, rather than advantages being defended to the bitter end. Early warnings are paid heed to, rather than ignored. Disengagement is seen as a way to free up and repurpose valuable resources rather than a dismaying signal of lost glory. Chapter 3, "Healthy Disengagement," explores this topic.

I asked Makiko Hamabe, Yahoo! Japan's head of investor relations, about how the company handles disengagement. She suggested that part of what allows this process to work for it is transparency in data about how people are using the service and how profitable it is. All the business heads, she explained, know how to look at traffic numbers to see what is profitable and what isn't and can also understand when a business creates conflict with key customers. At that point, the decision to exit is well understood and accepted, and people move on to other opportunities.

"Using Resource Allocation to Promote Deftness" (chapter 4) gets at the huge difference a world of transient advantage implies for how you manage assets and how you organize. Access to assets, not ownership of assets, will be a big theme. Assets that are variable and multiuse will in many cases be seen as more attractive than those that are fixed and dedicated. Preventing resources from being held hostage by the leaders of a particular advantage will become more standard as firms become aware of the dangers of a leader hanging on to an old advantage for too long.

One would think that construction and management of large projects would be about as rigid and hierarchical as it gets. And yet ACS's CEO Florentino Perez maintains that "constructing firms have diversified into activities requiring the same culture as that of the contractor . . . entering services, infrastructure, concessions and more recently, energy." ACS was cited as having a pivotal role to play in the restructuring of several sectors in Spain, diversifying into both new industries and new geographies, building flexibility into how those sectors are served now.[12]

"Building an Innovation Proficiency" (chapter 5) suggests that in a world of temporary advantage, innovation needs to be a continuous, core, well-managed process rather than the episodic and tentative process it is in many companies. An experimental orientation that is open to struggle and the odd failure, a defined process for managing each innovation phase, and career paths for innovators are all likely developments.

HDFC Bank, a rapidly growing Indian bank, stresses the importance of making innovation systematic and something that is on the leadership agenda. As its CEO, Aditya Puri, describes,

"We plan our growth across three horizons: one that I can see in front of me; second, what I can see in front of me but will become a big business five years from now; third, at the bottom of the pyramid, which will become a big business, maybe five years from now."[13]

Competing in volatile markets has implications for the mind-set leaders bring to their businesses, a topic explored in chapter 6. As the pace of competition becomes faster, decisions that are made quickly and in "roughly right" mode are likely to beat a decision-making process that is more precise, but slower. Prediction and being "right" will be less important than reacting quickly and taking corrective action. And unlike most corporate decision-making processes today, in which people seek out information that suggests they are correct, in a world of transient advantage the most valuable information is often disconfirming—it helps highlight where the greatest risks in being wrong are.

Tales of how hard-headed and candid the leaders in the growth outlier companies are are legendary. Take Cognizant and its CEO, Francisco D'Souza. If former CEO Lakshmi Narayanan is to be believed, there isn't even a hint of complacency in the way D'Souza sifts through a plan. Says Narayanan, "Any recommendation that goes to him will be challenged. The conclusion will be challenged, the reasoning behind the conclusion will be challenged, the data that supports the reasoning will be challenged, and the source of the data will be challenged. And, on a bad day, the methods and motives of the source will be challenged ... [I]t makes everyone think and look at alternatives dispassionately."[14] HDFC Bank's Aditya has a similar approach: "I tell people, please treat the CEO visit as a dentist visit. There will be pain. While you will get a lot of encouragement, my job is to tell you what's working and what is not."[15]

Finally, chapter 7 will consider what all this means for you, whether you are a leader, an employee, a client, or simply an observer of the scene. One reality is that we are starting to see a two-part world. For some people, the end of competitive advantage is going to mean painful downward adjustments in what they can aspire to at work because they don't possess rare or valuable skills. They are likely to be vulnerable to organizations' ruthlessly trimming fixed costs to maximize their own flexibility. For people with valuable, rare, or in-demand skills, however, the rewards are likely to be rich indeed. This last chapter of the book discusses how you should be thinking about your personal career strategy in light of transient advantages.

Before going further, you may want to assess your company's strategy. Are you trapped in an aging competitive advantage? Are you competing based on outdated assumptions? Find out with the assessment tool in the sidebar. And then enjoy learning how other firms have overcome the challenges.

Assessment

Is Your Company Trapped in a Competitive Advantage?

Good companies can be trapped into aging advantages and be surprised when things change. The diagnostic in table 1-4 can help pinpoint areas in which you might be at risk of being blindsided and suggest changes that you might want to make. Simply position your organization's current way of working on the scale between the two statements in the assessment. Those areas that fall to the left of the scale are the ones you might want to take a good hard look at.

TABLE 1-4

Our organization's current way of working

Focused on extending existing advantages	Scale	Capable of coping with transient advantages
Budget, people, and other resources are largely controlled by heads of established businesses.	1 2 3 4 5 6 7	Critical resources are controlled by a separate group from those who run businesses.
We tend to extend our established advantages if we possibly can.	1 2 3 4 5 6 7	We tend to move out of an established advantage early, with the goal of moving on to something new.
We don't have a systematic process for disengaging from a business.	1 2 3 4 5 6 7	We have a systematic way of exiting businesses.
Disengagements tend to be painful and difficult.	1 2 3 4 5 6 7	Disengagements are just part of the normal business cycle.
We try to avoid failures, even in uncertain situations.	1 2 3 4 5 6 7	We recognize that failures are unavoidable and try to learn from them.
We budget annually or for even longer.	1 2 3 4 5 6 7	We budget in quick cycles, either quarterly or on a rolling basis.
We like to stick to plans once they are formulated.	1 2 3 4 5 6 7	We are comfortable with changing our plans as new information comes in.
We emphasize optimization in our approach to asset utilization.	1 2 3 4 5 6 7	We emphasize flexibility in our approach to asset utilization.
Innovation is an on-again, off-again process.	1 2 3 4 5 6 7	Innovation is systematic, a core process for us.
It is difficult for us to pull resources from a successful business to fund more uncertain opportunities.	1 2 3 4 5 6 7	It is quite normal for us to pull resources from a successful business to fund more uncertain opportunities.
Our best talent spends most of their time solving problems and handling crises.	1 2 3 4 5 6 7	Our best talent spends most of their time working on new opportunities for our organization.
We try to keep our organizational structure relatively stable and to fit new ideas into the existing structure.	1 2 3 4 5 6 7	We reorganize when new opportunities require a different structure.
We tend to emphasize analysis over experimentation.	1 2 3 4 5 6 7	We tend to emphasize experimentation over analysis.
It isn't easy to be candid with our senior leaders when something goes wrong.	1 2 3 4 5 6 7	We find it very easy to be candid with senior leaders when something goes wrong.

2

Continuous Reconfiguration: Achieving Balance between Stability and Agility

The reconfiguration process is the secret sauce of remaining relevant in a situation of temporary advantage, because it is through reconfiguration that assets, people, and capabilities make the transition from one advantage to another (table 2-1). Because this is quite different from the thinking in conventional strategy, I thought it would make a suitable point of departure for the rest of the book. Organizations that get this right are shape shifters. You don't see dramatic downsizings or restructurings, you don't see people sticking with one role for long periods of time, and you don't see

TABLE 2-1

The new strategy playbook: reconfiguration

From	To
Extreme downsizing and restructuring	Continuous morphing and changing
Bulk of emphasis on arenas in exploitation phase	Equal emphasis on all phases of a competitive life cycle within an arena
Stability or dynamism alone	Stability combined with dynamism
Narrowly defined jobs and roles	Fluidity in allocation of talent
Stable vision, monolithic execution	Stable vision, variety in execution

confusion about the company's evolutionary path. Instead, there is a consistent reevaluation of current activities with the understanding that some may need to give way to new ones.

Continuous Morphing Rather Than Extreme Downsizing or Restructuring

A pattern to look for in organizations that have mastered transient-advantage environments is the continual freeing up of resources from old advantages in order to fund the development of new ones. For instance, Infosys moved its talent and people out of a business model that largely leveraged low-cost Indian labor into new business models that included services such as independent software testing and enterprise applications. Alan Mullally, the CEO of Ford Motor Company, announced that, although it would close its iconic Mercury brand (which went from selling 580,000 cars in its peak year, 1978, to just 92,000 in 2009), it would plow the resources freed up into its Lincoln and other brands. Telephone operator Verizon extracted resources from cash-generating but low-growth arenas such as telephone books and landlines to grow businesses based on fiber optic service technology (FIOS) and wireless connectivity.[1]

A fascinating case of a company that managed to overcome competitive forces that have decimated its entire industry is Milliken & Company, a privately held textile business. I was first introduced to the company by a participant in one of my courses at Columbia. He talked about "Mr. Milliken," the company's then-CEO, with a fervor usually reserved for cult figures or rock stars. Upon studying the company, it becomes clear why their leader inspired such enthusiasm. All of Milliken's traditional competitors have vanished, victims of a surge in global competition that essentially moved the entire business of textile manufacturing to Asia—by 1991, 58 percent of all fabric and apparel sold at retail in the United States was imported.[2] Roger Milliken, who originally tried to stem the tide of imports with aggressive public relations and lobbying activities (indeed, he founded the influential "Crafted with Pride in the USA" campaign), eventually decided that the future lay in reconfiguration of the company's business.[3] It had a long history of innovative activities, beginning with the establishment of its first research center in 1958 and the adoption of management practices so innovative that the company routinely won awards for its cutting-edge ideas.

In Milliken, one sees very clearly the pattern of entering new, more promising arenas even as it disengages from older and exhausted ones. Although it eventually did exit most of its traditional textile lines, it did not do so suddenly. As foreign competition launched its assault on American markets in the 1980s and 1990s, Milliken engaged in a steady number of plant closures. Despite its efforts to modernize its plants and make them competitive, one sees a gradual withdrawal from those arenas, with seven plant closings in the 1980s, several more in the 1990s, two in 2003, another in 2008, and the disposal of an automotive body cloth division in 2009. Every effort was made, as best I can tell, to reallocate the workers who suffered as a result. At the same time, Milliken invested in international expansion, new technologies, and new markets, including forays into

FIGURE 2-1

Milliken's reconfiguration path

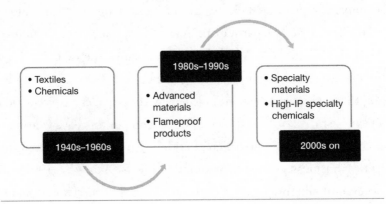

new arenas to which its capabilities gave access. As a favorable *Wall Street Journal* article observed in January 2012, "Milliken makes the fabric that reinforces duct tape, the additives that make refrigerator food containers clear and children's art markers washable, the products that make mattresses fire resistant, countertops antimicrobial, windmills lighter and combat gear protective."[4]

Visually, you can think of Milliken's reconfiguration path along the lines shown in figure 2-1. At the same time, Milliken prided itself on maintaining a legendary corporate culture, heavy on training and internal development, employee engagement, and deep pride in the company's accomplishments. If Milliken could transform its model from textiles to high-technology, there is hope for other organizations facing decline as well.

Escaping the Competitive Advantage Trap

Reed Hastings, the CEO of Netflix, has been pilloried in the business press for making a couple of reconfiguration moves that infuriated customers.[5] The first was a big price increase in the summer of 2010. The idea was to give Netflix enough cash flow to acquire more content as well as to cover the costs of shipping DVDs in a world going increasingly digital. The resulting furor had many subscribers desert the company. That move was followed by one that caused over half a million to abandon ship—a decision to split the streaming and DVD services into two separate companies. The new, streaming-oriented part of the firm would continue under the Netflix name. The DVD business would be dubbed "Qwickster" and would have its own website, corporate structure, and separate management. That idea made customers so angry that Hastings joked at a weekend off-site meeting that he probably should get a food taster. A speedy retreat ensued, with the idea for the Qwickster service dropped.

Although there is much to be critical about in the way these decisions were handled and communicated, the Netflix story illustrates a fundamental dilemma when competitive advantages shift: What do you do when the early warning signs of an eroding advantage make themselves known? How do you reconfigure the organization to simultaneously disengage from the original advantage while moving resources into the next one?

In the case of Netflix, Hastings is convinced that streaming is going to be the preferred vehicle for users to access content, whatever device they happen to use to do this. The DVD business, by extension, is not going to be the core of Netflix's future destiny. If you believe this, parting the two areas makes sense. The job of the Netflix leadership would be to manage rapid growth and access to digital content, whereas the job of the Qwickster leadership would be to manage the business for profits for as long as it lasts and squeeze economies out of it. Two contradictory activities. From a company point of view, it makes perfect sense.

Here's the problem, though. From a customer point of view, the switch was infuriating. Customers were used to populating their "queues" of movies and other content in one place, and were enraged at the idea that they would be required to duplicate that effort if they continued to want access to both formats. Further, the movie choices in the DVD area were vastly richer than those available to stream, creating even more frustration because users would need to check both places to see where they could get what they were looking for. And content providers, wary of Netflix proving disruptive to things such as expensive cable television subscriptions, were not particularly interested in Netflix's streaming offering being competitive with their networks.

The verdict is still out. To me, although the move to reduce dependence on the DVD business makes sense over the long haul, it was attempted too quickly. Critical though one might be of the DVD-to-streaming transition, Netflix is managing transitions in other realms with more skill. It has, for instance, reduced its dependence on movies to begin to offer television shows and even original programming. We'll have a look at how Netflix might have managed disengagement from the DVD business more gracefully in the next chapter.

Growth Outliers: Equal Emphasis on the Entire Wave Rather Than Focus on Exploitation Alone

Some firms seem to be able to manage business model transitions with reasonable grace. Recall the growth outliers from the opening chapter, a rare group of ten firms, out of nearly five thousand, that had managed to maintain steady growth rates despite huge upheavals in markets, economies, and industries in the period from 1999 to 2009 (table 2-2). A major conclusion from this study is that this group of firms had identified and implemented ways of combining tremendous internal stability while motivating tremendous external agility, particularly in terms of business models. Let's consider how they—and other companies 'with good track records of navigating from advantage to advantage—combine stability with dynamism.

TABLE 2-2

The growth outliers

Growth outlier	Industry	Head- quarters country	Founding year	Market capitaliza- tion (USD MM), year ending 2009	Number of employees (2009)
Infosys	IT consulting and other services	India	1981	$31,894	113,800
Yahoo! Japan	internet software and services	Japan	1996	$20,334	4,882
HDFC Bank	Diversified banks	India	1994	$16,554	51,888
ACS (Active- dades Con- struccion y Servicios)	Construction and engi- neering	Spain	1983	$15,525	142,176
Cognizant Technology Solutions	IT consulting and other services	United States	1994	$13,312	78,400
Tsingtao Brewery	Brewers	China	1903	$7,214	33,839
Indra Sistemas	IT consulting and other services	Spain	1921	$3,666	26,175
Krka dd Novo Mesto	Pharmaceu- ticals	Slovenia	1954	$3,186	7,975
FactSet	Application software	United States	1978	$3,009	4,116
Atmos Energy Corporation	Gas utilities	United States	1906	$2,614	4,913

Sources of Stability

Although dynamism and rapid change are all around us, people are not very effective when facing extreme uncertainty—it tends to be paralyzing. The outliers, therefore, have crafted social architectures that bound the amount of uncertainty and change their people have to face. Indeed, in the outlier companies, employees actually spent less time worrying about organizational roles and structures than people in many of the typical organizations I've worked with.

Ambition

Common to the outlier firms was a public commitment to world-class ambition, coupled with a clear sense of strategic direction in every case. This is reflected in the reviews given to them by analysts and external observers as reference companies. It's almost tedious to read the descriptions: the phrases "well managed," "best prac-tices," and "benchmarks" come up over and over again. Relative to competitors, their leadership appears to have outsize ambition, which sets the bar high. Their leadership also promotes common key themes that are the result of a compelling strategy diagnosis. At Infosys, for instance, the leaders talk about Infosys 1.0 (basically labor-arbitrage), Infosys 2.0 (global expansion into services), and now the emergence of Infosys 3.0.

HDFC Bank was founded with the explicit intention of becom-ing a truly global Indian bank with best-practice standards in all of its operations. As its website proclaims, "HDFC Bank began opera-tions in 1995 with a simple mission: to be a 'World-class Indian Bank'. We realised that only a single-minded focus on product quality and service excellence would help us get there." At Infosys, the founding team was determined to create a modern Indian com-pany with transparent and globally acceptable practices (its CEO was recognized in 2009 as one of the fifty most influential management thinkers in the world by Thinkers50, a management award). Cognizant was "born global" as an offshoot of Dun & Bradstreet and built ambitious growth targets into its strategy from the start. Krka is ambitiously expanding far from its Eastern European roots, with investments and partnerships across the globe (including partnerships in China and other countries to support the expansion of its capabilities). Atmos Energy set itself the goal of achieving world-class efficiency in the regulated part of its gas generation business and steady growth in its unregulated units. ACS proudly notes that it is "a world reference in the promotion, development, construction and management of infrastructures and services of all types."[6]

Unsurprisingly, references to awards and recognition are to be found liberally festooning the companies' corporate websites. HDFC Bank features an entire *section* dedicated to awards. It lists thirty-four awards for 2010 alone. Note the subtle symbolism: nobody in leadership would like to be in charge in a year for which no awards were listed. Infosys regularly places in the top of rankings such as *Fortune*'s Top 10 companies for leaders. FactSet has been featured in the *Fortune* 100 list of best companies to work for, *BusinessWeek*'s ranking of places to start a career, and so on. Indra Sistemas won *Computerworld*'s best service company award in 2007. It is also acknowledged as one of the world's "most ethical companies," an award it won in 2010 after a string of "most sustainable" awards. Krka proudly proclaims that it has won the Golden Otis Award of Trust for its products, an award in which consumers indicate which brands they trust most. The key point here is that the strategies for each of these companies were grounded in a compelling ambition for the firm, an ambition that provides an aiming point for their people.

The finding that stretch ambitions are important to long-term reconfiguration is consistent with what other observers have concluded is essential for preventing companies from becoming complacent and content to pursue yesterday's advantages. Mikko Kosonen, for instance, a long-time Nokia senior executive during its glory days and now a consultant and professor, argues that stretch, instability, and multidimensionality are crucial to keep a company from getting stuck. As he noted in an interview with me, "Stretch and contradictory goals are important," as are mechanisms to keep complacency at bay, such as moving people around to facilitate their looking at the business in different ways from different vantage points.

Identity and Culture

A second source of stability is the investment these firms make in creating a common identity, culture, and commitment to leadership development. They pay considerable attention to values, culture, and alignment. They also invest in training, training, and more training.

A recent MBA thesis examining the culture of HDFC Bank found that its employees generally scored the firm highly on cultural values such as organizational effectiveness, employee engagement, and a supportive culture.[7] At FactSet, the culture is promoted on its website as a key draw for potential employees to work with the firm. ACS's chairman in a recent annual report emphasized "recruiting and retaining the best talent" as one of four "vectors" for the firm's strategy. Bob Best, the then-CEO of Atmos Energy, decided in 1997 that the creation of culture and shared values was going to be a differentiator for the firm. As he put it, "I do think that creating the right foundation for your culture allows you to make changes as you need to make changes. Culture is the foundation for all success. This has been a very important process to the long-term health and success of our company."[8]

Deployment, Yes, but also Development

Another factor in play in companies that can move from one set of advantages to another is that they consciously set out to educate and up-skill their people. Kris Gopalakrishnan of Infosys explained that the company places a heavy emphasis on training. When I asked him how the company moves people from advantage to advantage, he said, "We hire for learnability—we deliberately select people for their capacity to learn new things." As he observes, at any given time Infosys has about 80 percent of its people deployed in some way, which is good because that is how it makes money. With the 20 percent of time that is not being used for deployment, employees are expected to take advantage of education and training opportunities so that their skills can be kept upgraded and they can potentially be moved from one kind of advantage to another. Infosys is famous for its Infosys Education Center, a $120 million facility that has the capacity to train 13,500 candidates at a time.

Smart companies recognize that continuous training and development is a mechanism to avoid having to fire people when competitive conditions shift, and they invest in training even as they pursue deployment. Take CLS Communication. This Swiss-based provider of language services was originally a spinoff of the in-house translation services of Swiss Bank Corporation and Zurich Financial Services in 1997. Since then, it has been growing rapidly, even as the underlying technologies for its core businesses of writing, editing, and translation have undergone tremendous shifts. I asked its CEO, Doris Albisser, how she handles the human side of business model and technology shifts. She emphasized continuous training and also moving people around the firm as needs changed. She mentioned training specifically in conjunction with the introduction of a new technology—machine translation coupled with text databases. Although her own people resisted adopting the new approach, they finally achieved a breakthrough when one of the more senior translators actually started training the others.

The point is that when you realize that shifts are inevitable, training people to be able to move from advantage to advantage becomes a cost of doing business. It's just as important a bill to pay as the one you pay to keep the lights on and the computers running. Investing in people's capacity to move around removes a tremendous barrier to change and suggests a redirection of emphasis from pure deployment to creating transition capability.

Strategy and Leadership

The stability of the outlier firms' strategy statements through the course of our study period is remarkable. This was a tumultuous time that began with the internet bubble bursting and included the tragedy of 9/11, the global housing and credit bubbles, the introduction of the euro, wars in Iraq and Afghanistan, the explosion of the internet as a vehicle for commerce, and the great recession of 2008. Yet, these firms appear not to have internalized the chaos in their environments. Interviews with their leaders are peppered with references to a few clear and simple strategic priorities, to the importance of building culture and developing talent, and to leveraging a few core capabilities. The CEOs and executive teams create a tremendous force for stability, even in the midst of major change.

At Tsingtao Brewery, for instance, despite the sudden death of its hard-driving CEO in 2001, subsequent leaders committed to following through on his international expansion strategy. The then-CEO of Spain's ACS at its 1983 founding expressed his commitment to making it Spain's most profitable public construction company. Today, that strategy continues with the company's stated objective of being a leader in "both civil and industrial engineering projects." Atmos Energy is today executing the strategy articulated by its former CEO in 1997, leveraging efficiency in its regulated business and driving growth in its unregulated businesses. FactSet's strategy statement has not changed at all since its founding, despite massive shifts in underlying technologies and an explosion of information relevant to its key clients.

Senior leadership at the companies was also for the most part stable. For all ten companies we studied, the current most senior executive was promoted from an internal position. There were no white knights and no outside-the-industry saviors. Interestingly, and also consistent with the findings of other researchers over the years, the most senior leaders generally kept a low profile. Although they were respected, acknowledged as having made major contributions, and were somewhat visible in the press, for the most part they were not high-profile public figures. The CEO of ACS is an exception, having showily purchased the Real Madrid soccer team and populated it with extremely expensive international talent. The five I have had the pleasure to meet in person were invariably low-key, courteous, and attentive to the comments of their conversation partners.

Stable Relationships

It is also noteworthy that the relationships among the outlier firms and their clients and ecosystem partners tend to be extremely stable as well. FactSet boasts that its client retention rate has been 95 percent over the past ten years, and on its website notes that it has a 90 percent employee retention rate. Analysts observe that both Infosys and Cognizant have strong client retention (with Cognizant boasting of a 90 percent client satisfaction rate on a recent survey, and Infosys reporting retention of 95 percent in a recent interview with us). Indra Sistemas observes in its annual report that "Indra

considers its suppliers and knowledge institutions to be partners in value creation and allies in innovation and that is a major
responsibility." This factor works together with our observation that
wrenching change seldom characterizes strategic shifts at the outlier companies—the fact that they can change in an evolutionary
manner as their customers change aligns the interests of clients and
service firms rather than pitting them against one another.

Other companies, too, have learned the value of preserving relationships. Interestingly, they take the issue of what happens to the
people who were engaged in an eroding advantage extremely seri-
ously and consciously manage the process. Nancy McKinstry, the
CEO of publisher Wolters Kluwer, had to confront this problem
often as the company made a difficult transition from largely print
outputs to a digital world. She emphasized redeployment from one
market to another and retraining as key to preserving flexibility
while keeping people.

Of course, it isn't always possible to redeploy or retrain people,
and sometimes a parting of the ways is necessary. What exemplary companies seem to do is to manage these separations in
such a way that those who have moved on maintain good relationships with the firm, even after they have been fired or laid
off. Cambridge consultancy Sagentia is practically a pure-play
transient-advantage firm because it has built fluidity, change, and
business model transition into its culture. Even it occasionally
needs to make people redundant, however. I asked one of its senior leaders about this, and he said that the company goes out of
its way to make sure that such staffing decisions are perceived as
fair and transparent. And what happened to the people? "Some
of them set up their own consultancy," he said. "Some got senior roles in the companies we used to do consulting for . . . The
important thing is that the people come to a good landing. I personally keep in touch with them."

So even in firms that embrace change and appear to manage it well, there are elements of tremendous stability in their businesses. How, then, do they preserve the dynamism that highly competitive markets require? To answer this question, one needs to look also at what *does* change. In other words, where do we see these firms behaving in a dynamic and agile way?

Sources of Agility

In contrast to the internal systems and structures that created stability over time in vision, strategy, culture, and leadership, I found equally well-developed and sophisticated approaches in these firms to fostering strategic agility—in other words, to sparking change routinely and consistently. The first such approach was a bit of a surprise—namely, that these firms, over the entire study period, had no dramatic downsizings, restructurings, or sell-offs.

Shape Shifting, Not Dramatic Restructuring

When I first started the outliers study, I expected to find that firms that were able to survive in spite of ephemeral advantages would have great processes for downsizing, restructuring, and otherwise getting out of declining areas in a big way. So I spent an entire summer torturing my student researchers to find instances of how these firms exited segments, canceled projects, or otherwise got out of business areas. The increasingly frustrated students searched in vain.

Instead, it seems that the outlier firms, relative to competitors, embed change in their normal routines. They reallocate resources flexibly and on an ongoing basis, rather than going through sudden divestitures or restructurings. Despite our best efforts, we found almost no instances of a sudden, wrenching exit. What we found instead was a tendency to redeploy resources and shift emphasis. We also noted that the firms seemed to accept industry evolution (especially regarding technologies) and embrace the changes in order to enter newer markets instead of cutting costs and divesting, just as we saw with Milliken. They use industry change as an opportunity to exit old businesses and enter new, higher-growth segments.

Alison Norman, one of my research assistants, observed that exit information for these firms was "elusive" and that the five companies she researched seemed to have a knack for integrating their old technologies into new waves, accepting the evolution of their industries but taking them into new markets rather than divesting completely. Xi Zhang, another researcher, came to the same conclusion, namely, that "instead of divestiture and disposal, they choose to *upgrade* in order to move up the value chain. Rapid upgrading is a common feature among all three companies [Infosys, HDFC, and FactSet] that I have researched."

Cognizant, during the period of our study, made nine strategic acquisitions but had no divestitures. The company itself was a spinoff from Dun & Bradstreet and began by offering straightforward technology services. Over the years it has moved into more professional consulting services and differentiated itself by a strong industry focus and co-location of its teams with its clients. As the company has evolved, it has shifted technology and people from low-growth businesses (such as plain-vanilla business process outsourcing) to more people-intensive, high-touch businesses, such as selling complete and complex software solutions. The company is pursuing a strategy that CEO Francisco D'Souza terms an evolution from labor arbitrage to intellectual arbitrage, and appears to be doing so without the wholesale downsizing that competitors such as Satyam Computer Services have experienced.

The interesting thing about how these companies exited areas is that they followed a far more evolutionary path than their competitors appeared to. Sanjay Purohit, the head of strategy for Infosys, explained it to me this way: "When we decide to get out of something, we slow down on allocating resources to those things. They find their way to insignificance in a period of time . . . You don't need to chop it off, you need to let it live its life . . . It's easy for us to repurpose the leadership and the talent, to look at some other area. We are a company that never fires its people. We transition the customers out of it, and people take other responsibilities." I thought that was a brilliantly succinct description of how a firm that is comfortable with transient advantage thinks.

Budgeting Is Fast, Flexible, and Not Held Hostage by Powerful Executives

One of the more subtle implications of this transformation-without-wrenching-change approach is that the firms manage major resource allocations centrally. This matters, because in many companies resources are trapped and, in the words of a friend of mine who is a chief strategy officer at a major multinational, "held hostage" at the divisional or business unit level. When a business is under pressure, or an opportunity falls between units, a company can be unable to respond effectively because incumbent executives regard the change as a threat. In the case of the outliers, decision making with respect to major strategic challenges appears to have been centrally coordinated, with considerable latitude for action at the business unit level. Budgeting also happens far more in real time than in many organizations.

At Infosys, for instance, budgets are adjusted on a rolling four-quarter basis. And, says Sanjay with a wicked grin, "I could rebudget the firm every seven days if I had to. I don't because it would drive people crazy, but we could." Infosys prides itself on being able to reallocate resources "at a very fast pace." Sanjay's function, which is corporate planning, does the recasting and reallocating. In a very transparent way, Infosys makes it obvious to everyone when a business doesn't need as many resources. Indeed, a business unit head might actually call Sanjay and ask to give some resources back because its business won't support that size this quarter. Can you imagine that conversation in a typical hierarchical company? High-quality data systems and absolute transparency help with the process. Sanjay tells me that there is no concept of hidden data in the company—everything is as transparent to the business units as it is to corporate, and there is only one version of the truth. "Our chairman has a great phrase for this," he says. "In God we trust, everybody else brings data."

I was struck by this—imagine a business unit leader in a typical company coming to the head of strategy and asking for resources to be taken away. It certainly doesn't happen in those cases in which people and assets under management are the measure of corporate importance.

Flexibility

Just as in budgeting, a factor that appears to support the shape-shifting approach to change is that our outlier firms make considerable investments in flexibility. So rather than heavy annual budgeting processes and efficiency-oriented values, the outlier firms invest in increasing their flexibility, even if this might lead to a small degree of suboptimization. Krka, for instance, has among its five core values "speed and flexibility" (the others are partnership and trust, creativity and efficiency). It goes so far as to create an annual award in which the employees who best exemplify these attributes are rewarded.

At the outlier companies, adjustments to strategy and changes in resource allocation were not annual exercises. They were far more likely to be quarterly. This applies to promotions and personnel evaluations as well. At Yahoo! Japan, for instance, Makiko Hamabe, the head of investor relations, described a quarterly target and evaluation system, combined with a 360-degree evaluation that would determine whether a person would be promoted or not.

The interesting aspect of the way these companies work is that the accelerated pace of their operations allows them to be extremely responsive to changes in the environment, catching the need to make changes and adapt earlier than companies with a more rigid, annual process. They also appear to have dealt with a major barrier to effective change, which is the fear and sense of career risk that often leads managers to cling to eroding businesses long after they should have moved on.

Innovation Is the Norm, Not the Exception

All too often in companies intent on exploitation, innovation is an afterthought. In the outlier companies, rather than innovation being an episodic, on-again, off-again endeavor, innovation is continuous, mainstream, and part of everyone's job. Innovation and the opportunity recognition process appear unendingly on the companies' websites, feature in their recruitment materials, and are reinforced by investment. All of the firms proudly list how much they are investing in new activities such as R&D or international expansion. It is also worth noting that these companies have processes for managing the entire innovation pipeline that cut across business units.

At Yahoo! Japan, for example, Hamabe explained that the company is pursuing four growth strategies: first, what it calls "Yahoo! everywhere," which is to facilitate access to the site from any kind of device; next, user-oriented social media, which means adding information from users to other data that can be found on the Yahoo! Japan site to make it more valuable; third, personalized local information that focuses on developing offerings for specific individuals based on their interests and needs; and finally, open network partnerships, which seek to offer businesses solutions to problems such as accepting online payments. Within each of these areas, managers are regularly given opportunities to identify where they think the next set of promising opportunities will be, coupled with a process of dedicating resources to the opportunities that appear most compelling. At the same time, the company's leaders continually monitor the usage of key services and their impact on relations with key partners to determine when a service should no longer be offered.

At Infosys, every unit is tasked by the senior executive team every year with articulating two big things they are going to do that will dramatically and in real time move their business forward—and to go public with that declaration. It is continuously thinking of new things as part of everybody's "day job." FactSet prides itself on "thirty years of innovations" and goes so far as to declare its ability to innovate a critical competitive factor in its 2008 10-K filing with the government.[9] Tsingtao Brewery is recognized among Chinese companies for its continuous innovations. As one former CEO said in announcing a change of direction toward greater integration, "We must not try to become large in order to become powerful. We must become powerful in order to become large." A recent focus of its innovative efforts has been a thrust in the direction of environmentally responsible brewing. As a local journal reports, "Years of hard work paid off. Tsingtao Beer has topped its rivals on the list of 'China Green Companies Top 100' at the Annual Summit of China Green Companies 2010, held in Chengdu, Sichuan Province this April."[10]

An Options-Oriented Pattern to Market Exploration

I showed an early version of this chapter to my coauthor and colleague Ian MacMillan, and he observed that the options-oriented approach we've been studying for some time seems to fit very well with how these firms think about opportunities. As he put it, "It's like building a firm that grazes on options—always testing, then engaging and entering, then disengaging from exhausted areas well before disengagement becomes costly." What the new strategy playbook seeks to embed is a mind-set and set of management processes that cultivate this pattern.

Relative to competing firms, the firms in our sample appeared to share an options-oriented pattern to exploring new opportunities. The essence of this approach is that they make small initial investments to explore opportunities, following up later with more substantial investments as the opportunity warrants. They are also willing to abandon a particular initiative if it doesn't appear to be developing effectively. Overall, the firms tended to move earlier than competitors into spaces that appeared attractive, even if their ultimate market size was not clear. Further, the firms seemed to be more active overall in pursuing a constant stream of new initiatives.

HDFC Bank's history of entering into various new growth markets is illustrative. In 1998, it joined the Cirrus alliance so that Mastercard holders worldwide could use the bank's ATM network. It then became the first bank in India to launch an international debit card in association with Visa in 2001. This was followed by innovations in credit card utilization such as credit cards specifically for farmers and later a 2007 agreement with Tata Pipes to offer credit facilities for farmers. In contrast, ICICI Bank, a key competitor, only began exploring internationally linked debit cards in 2000. HDFC Bank followed a similar pattern of moving early and building from initial success in many other new markets, including linking to worldwide ATM networks, providing telebanking services, mobile banking, consumer loans (such as financing for car radios), e-commerce, wholesale banking, online accounting services, and foreign exchange services. Indeed, the only market in which a competitor seems to have beaten HDFC to capitalizing on a growth market was in the Indian rural market, in which the State Bank of India already had a well-established position. HDFC's response was characteristic: the firm linked up with the Postal Department to extend its reach and offered innovative products such as market linkage programs for self-help groups (self-help groups are composed typically of women who each contribute a small amount of money on a regular basis until there is enough to make a loan, which can go to members or to other investments). In addition, the firm prides itself on its emphasis on experimentation and continuous innovation.

A reporter, examining HDFC's long run of success, observed that CEO Puri is "a cautious banker" who enters new areas deliberately, through a process of learning, adapting, proving viability, and then expanding into category after category. As Puri says, "Personal loans, gold loans, microfinance, two-wheelers, crop loans—it's been the same, deliberate process."[11]

In contrast to their competitors, the outlier firms also appeared to have fewer big, high-risk all-or-nothing bets, which is also consistent with an options orientation. In comparing Indra Sistemas with competitor BAE Systems, for instance, although both firms made acquisitions and had disposals during the study period, those of BAE tended to be larger—most of Indra's acquisitions were under $100 million, whereas most of BAE's were well over that amount, with one enormous $4.5 billion acquisition (of Armor Holdings in 2007). Kris Gopalakrishnan, the former CEO of Infosys, told me that the company would never engage in a merger worth more than 10 percent of its revenues, in order to limit the downside cultural and business risks.

Finally, the companies had diverse, but related, portfolios. Each of the companies appeared to maintain enough diversity in its portfolio that it could simultaneously invest in the renewal of its core businesses while exploring new alternatives. Their consistent performance is partly a reflection of the fact that when one segment goes into decline, others can be leveraged. Indra Sistemas, for example, was able to leverage diversification moves from its defense businesses into computer systems designs with the acquisitions of BDE and into banking by buying Diagrama FIP. Through subsequent acquisitions, it was able to build and maintain a formidable solutions portfolio without being overly dependent on one business model or end market. Even in the case of the two single-product companies, Tsingtao Brewery and Yahoo! Japan, diversity in terms of geographic reach (Tsingtao) and diversity of services offered and segments served (Yahoo! Japan) appeared to honor this principle.

The Paradoxical Combination of Stability and Agility in Continuous Reconfiguration

I undertook the outliers study with the hope of gaining some insight into how firms can persist, grow, and even thrive when specific competitive advantages are transient. A major conclusion I have come to from this research is that these companies navigate seemingly incompatible demands deftly.

On the one hand, they exhibit tremendous stability. Their values, cultural norms, core strategies, capabilities, customer relationships, and leadership are remarkably consistent over time. Although they do change and adapt, the changes are evolutionary, and the adaptations rapid and generally modest. They put serious investment into "soft" factors such as training and reinforcing their corporate values, which are backed up by meaningful symbolic actions on the part of their leaders.

Against this platform of stability, however, is a tremendous amount of experimentation and innovation. The firms are developing and deploying new technologies, moving into new markets, exploring new business models, and even opening up new industries. They take on acquisitions and aggressively seek to obtain external inputs from people and organizations not at all like their own. They rapidly adjust and readjust resources and are comfortable with moving executives and staff from one role to another.

Rather than being contradictory, as an initial look might suggest, the twin abilities to maintain coherence and alignment while at the same time innovating and challenging the status quo are deeply interdependent. A stable organizational environment with transparent values is conducive to employees' feeling confident that they can take the risks that experimentation requires. Norms of high performance and "reference company" ambitions prevent stability from degrading into complacency. Strong values enforced symbolically help maintain reasonable ethical standards. Continual small changes refresh the organization and keep it from becoming stale, while at the same time avoiding the "big bang" risks of massive restructuring. Continuity of management allows for the formation of informal internal networks, which research has long shown are associated with successful innovation. Consistent corporate rhythms and internal practices free up time and energy for doing new things that would otherwise be spent sorting out how old ones should be happening.

The leadership and management challenge is thus maintaining an organizational system that can maintain the complementarity between the forces for innovation and those for stability. Too heavy a shift in the direction of innovation, and corporate coherence and the benefits of integration break down. Too heavy a shift in the direction of stability, and innovation and change can suffer. In either case, what made the difference in our study was not the "hard" analytical issues such as capital structure, cost of capital, prices of assets, or market capitalization.

This chapter on reconfiguration provides a fairly high-level look at what it takes to thrive when competitive advantages come and go. In the chapters that follow we will dig more deeply into core processes. Next, we'll take a look at how healthy disengagement from a declining line of business actually works.

3

Healthy Disengagement

Texts on strategy and innovation are full of great ideas of new things that leaders should do. But, lamented a senior executive I was with recently, "There aren't any textbooks on what to *stop* doing!" In a world of temporary advantage, stopping things—exiting declining advantages—is every bit as critical as starting things. Activities need to stop because they can no longer demonstrate good growth potential, or perhaps competitors have made them a commodity, or perhaps they simply have few growth prospects.

In the last chapter, we explored how the growth outlier firms use a process of continuous small changes to avoid having to make more substantive exit and disengagement decisions. But not all firms are so fortunate—there are some occasions in which a more radical disengagement is simply necessary. This could be because a declining business drops off faster than expected (as happened to Fuji Photo in the 1990s), because markets change in a radical way (as happened to the smartphone business with the introduction

THE END OF COMPETITIVE ADVANTAGE

TABLE 3-1

The new strategy playbook: disengagement

From	To
Defending an advantage to the bitter end	Ending advantages frequently, formally, and systematically
Exits viewed as strategically undesirable	Emphasis on retaining learning from exits
Exits occur unexpectedly and with great drama	Exits occur in a steady rhythm
Focus on objective facts	Focus on subjective early warnings

of the iPhone), or simply because a firm lingers a little too long in the "exploit" phase and didn't reconfigure. This chapter tackles that topic (table 3-1).

Early Warnings of Decline: What Do You Look For?

Evidence that a business or business model is going into decline is usually quite clear long before it creates a corporate crisis. If one is interested in looking, there is usually a lot of good information to be found. The trouble is that this information seldom turns up in the routine measurements companies use to drive their businesses.

Diminishing Returns to Innovation

The first clear warning sign is when next-generation innovations offer smaller and smaller improvements in the user experience. If the people designing the next-generation offer are having trouble conceiving of new ways to differentiate what you do, that's not good. If your scientists and engineering types are predicting that some new discovery will undermine the existing trajectory, that is also not good. For instance, RIM's BlackBerry e-mail devices were the natural descendants of the first pagers, with keypads. The trajectory on which they developed didn't change much, adding mostly incremental touches such as colored screens, cameras, voice recorders, and some applications. Although customers appreciated these innovations, they were no longer excited by them.

Increasing Commoditization

A second clear warning sign is when you start to hear customers saying that new alternatives are increasingly acceptable to them. Or worse, that cheaper alternatives are just as good as what you have to offer and that there is little differentiation between them. For example, Google has developed a maps application for Android-equipped mobile phones that provides turn-by-turn spoken navigation. This has prompted a decline in the attractiveness of standalone GPS navigation devices, and even predictions that such devices will no longer be popular in automobile dashboards or as handhelds.

Even worse is when a competitive or substitute offering shows the threat of changing the dimensions of competition customers are looking for, particularly if it comes as a surprise. Just recently, an insider reported on the reaction at RIM with respect to the 2007 introduction of the iPhone:

> RIM, as well as Motorola, Nokia, Palm and other early pioneers, lost ground partly because of a self-defeating attitude. RIM in particular assumed from the start that smartphones would be outgrowths of its pagers and that there would never be enough battery life or wireless technology for more functions. It started growing beyond this view before the iPhone shipped, but the OS foundation until recently was based on the early assumption.

The remarks confirm a widely held belief that BlackBerry Storm development started only after the iPhone was made public rather than having been in development at all before. RIM didn't have its first touchscreen phone until the Storm shipped in late 2008, almost two years after the iPhone's unveiling, and didn't have multi-touch support or a fully accurate web browser until the Torch arrived just this past summer.[1]

RIM, in a frantic catch-up position on features customers now say they want (and which are offered at very competitive prices on Android phones at least), is fighting to combat market share declines.

Diminishing Returns to Capital Employment

Finally, of course, you can consult your numbers. The first thing that usually happens is a small decline in the sales growth rate. Then a flattening out. Then eventually declining sales. Unfortunately, by the time a decline shows up in your performance numbers, it is usually too late to muster a proactive response, and you find yourself clambering back in a weaker position than you had been in.

At Wolters Kluwer, a once-traditional publishing company navigating a transformation to the digital world, managing the portfolio of products is a skill the company has honed very well. With products that still have some life cycle to them, the company manages by "pruning," as CEO McKinstry notes. Updates might be a little less frequent, and fewer editorial resources might be dedicated. This is considered "harvesting" and has been readily adopted as part of the way in which publishing life cycles are managed. Far more difficult is the challenge of an outright divestiture. In her company, McKinstry has instituted a review that "organizes micro markets by category." Anything growing organically more than 5 percent is considered to be high growth and will continue to be supported. Growth in the 2 percent to 5 percent range is considered "maintain." Growth below 2 percent is a candidate for harvest, and failing that, for divestiture. One of McKinstry's innovations since taking the reins at Wolters Kluwer was to implement a more structured portfolio review process, with the result that today "more than 60 percent of our capital is going into markets that are growing more than 5 percent," as she told me in an interview. She attributes this discipline regarding managing the portfolio as helpful to "divesting from more things than we would have done" before shifting the analytical emphasis.

Who Makes the Exit Decision?

It is unrealistic to expect that managers whose careers and future prospects depend on "their" business continuing will put up their hands and suggest that a disengagement might be appropriate. Indeed, all the skills of increasing efficiency and deepening customer loyalty that are so valuable during the period of exploitation can make a business that really should be a candidate for disengagement look attractive for a rather long time. Further, at many companies, information that might lead to questions about a business or division is not aggregated or presented in such a way that the decision is without question. There seem to be three ways of overcoming this challenge. The first is to set up an ongoing, dedicated team to regularly go through the firm's portfolio and identify candidates for disengagement or divestiture, as Wolters Kluwer has done. The second is to aggressively and frequently change the management team, a pattern found by consultancy Accenture.[2] The third is for the CEO to drive regular evaluations of what should be in and out of the business's portfolio, a challenge that A. G. Lafley of Procter & Gamble defined as "linking the outside to the inside" of a business. As he argues in an article in *Harvard Business Review*, "only the CEO has the enterprisewide perspective to make the tough choices involved."[3]

As I mentioned in chapter 1, at Yahoo! Japan (one of the outliers), Makiko Hamabe, the head of investor relations, echoes this thought: "Our CEO says that he is his own heaviest user and as a user he doesn't want Yahoo! Japan to do something that annoys him. That's the basic idea." This connection to the business allows him to drive a relatively dispassionate numbers-based evaluation of what offerings Yahoo! Japan should pursue and which it should abandon. In that company, key reasons for disengagement are when usage and profitability are low, or if a service creates conflicts with other businesses. A conflict might prompt a discontinuation of the service. As Hamabe continued, "Our management team will discontinue a business when they see that profitability is low, or maybe it has a conflict with other businesses. For example, several years ago we stopped offering videocast. It was like YouTube in that people can upload videos. But as you know, on YouTube you have a lot of non-licensed unofficial videos. So we have instead a service like Hulu (we call it Yell). It's also a video service, but the content is authorized." The videocast business was deemed to be incompatible with good relations with content producers and was ended.

Not All Final Curtains Are the Same

Tolstoy wrote a memorable phrase that some wags have dubbed the "Anna Karenina principle"—namely, "All happy families are alike, while all unhappy families are unhappy in their own way." So too with a competitive advantage that has faded: not all are the same, not all suggest the same outcome, and not all will end badly. Over time, statistically, most businesses lose value. Indeed, some years ago in their book *Creative Destruction*, then-McKinsey researchers Richard Foster and Sarah Kaplan found that as a business aged, its total return to shareholders, relative to its industry, declined systematically.[4] A later article in *Harvard Business Review* basically makes the point that if you think you have a candidate for divestiture or otherwise ramping down, you should move quickly because the passage of time will destroy any remaining value rapidly.[5]

Here, however, we are contemplating the problem that is sometimes unavoidable: when a former business creating competitive advantage ought to be removed from the corporate portfolio. This can be for any of three reasons. First, you may have concluded, as Netflix has, that your current core offering is becoming obsolete for some reason and you need to transition customers, suppliers, and the organization to some new platform. Second, a business might actually have strong cash flow and be attractive as a going concern, but it no longer fits your strategy. Or finally, a business or capability may simply be heading into obsolescence. Next, we have the question of time—some shifts in advantage are relatively evolutionary and give you quite a bit of time to work with. Others happen so quickly that immediate action is essential. If we combine these elements, we can think of six different types of disengagement activities.

Different Strategies for Disengagement

The first dimension concerns the judgment of management about the future of an asset or capability. The second concerns the extent to which there is substantial time pressure to enact the disengagement, yielding the simple matrix shown in table 3-2.

TABLE 3-2

Disengagement strategies

	Capability is core to the future of the business	Capability has value, but not for us	Capability is in decline
Relatively little time pressure	**Orderly migration** Transition aspects of the business from today's configuration to tomorrow's	**Garage sale** Get reasonable prices for assets we are no longer interested in	**Run-off** Be well paid to maintain support for customers while decreasing investment
Intense time pressure	**Hail Mary** Divest formerly core capabilities and find a solution to migrate to the new core fast	**Fire sale** Sell noncore assets we are no longer in a position to exploit	**Last man standing** Spark consolidation or otherwise try for a profitable end-game position

Orderly Migration: Customers' Needs Are Going to Be Met in a New Way, but You Have Time

I first ran across the remarkable story of Norway's Schibsted in a 2010 *BusinessWeek* article.[6] Schibsted is a newspaper publisher, a venerable institution founded in 1839. Like newspaper publishers everywhere, it is coping with a staggering loss of ad revenue. The *BusinessWeek* article noted that US newspapers' ad revenues collapsed catastrophically in the years between 2000 and 2010, from $48.6 billion in 2000 to $24.8 billion in 2009, with classified ads suffering the greatest declines. Like their American brethren, Schibsted's newspapers, dailies such as *VG* and *Aftenposten*, have seen their revenue from advertising, particularly classified ads, collapse. Unlike their American cousins, however, Schibsted doesn't care at all. As it turns out, most of the customer defections are going from Schibsted-owned companies to . . . well, a Schibsted-owned company. In 1999, the company spun off an online business called FINN.no that provides a platform for online advertising. It competes directly with the papers, and as far as CEO Rolv Erik Ryssdal is concerned, that's just fine with him. "We weren't afraid to cannibalize ourselves," he told a reporter.[7]

The online business model Schibsted pursues isn't all that different from that of Craigslist, the scourge of the American newspaper executive. Most listings are available for free. The company charges a premium to give listings more visibility, and Schibsted's site also carries listings from businesses, which Craigslist does not. It has sister sites that operate job-search and automotive sales operations. Operating costs for both are minimal, with the consequence that the online ads are more profitable than the print ads ever were. The Norwegians have taken their show on the road, opening advertising sites in twenty-two countries either through acquisition or through greenfield development. The company is now the world's number three player in online advertising, behind Craigslist and eBay. Profit margins at some of its sites are reported to be 60 percent.

Kjell Aamot, the CEO who preceded Ryssdal, is widely regarded in Scandinavia as a visionary, and was one of the longest-tenured CEOs of publicly traded companies headquartered in the region. He rather unpopularly predicted the demise of the current print-newspaper model "within 20 years," prompting one observer to complain that "we are getting pretty tired of all these predictions of the end of the newspaper business."[8] Where does he get his inspiration? From, among other places, his grandchildren. An observer of the print media described Aamot's conclusions about the future: he saw that his grandchildren were watching less television, preferring instead to use the internet and mobile phones. He was also startled at how often they changed their habits—moving from interactive real-time games to something else. He definitely saw that traditional newspapers were a poor fit for their needs.[9] Amidst a career filled with controversies, Aamot was the main driver behind the move to internet properties for the company, helping it prepare for the erosion of its primary business model. And the future? Perhaps, he points out, journalism will be paid for from subsidies originating from other businesses, such as car sales.

The Schibsted story is illustrative of how one can disengage from a business by gradually migrating customers, revenue streams, and operating models from the old advantage to a new one. It is also an interesting take on reverse customer adoption. Those customers who wanted to go online found a ready vehicle for doing so and converted early. Those who didn't want to work this way weren't forced to do so until they were ready. The migration from early adopters through the mass market was managed pretty skillfully by Schibsted.

Not so much for Netflix. By forcing a transition on customers before many of them were ready, the company enraged them. Rather than figuring out which segments should be exited, and doing so sequentially, Netflix attempted the same strategy for everybody all at once. The result was that the mass market went up in arms. What I think it should have done was realize that preparing customers for transitions is just like getting them through the new product adoption process, except in reverse. Not all customers are going to be prepared to move at the same rate. There is a sequence to which customers you should transition away from first, which next, and so on.

If Reed Hastings had, instead of raising prices for everybody, selectively offered price discounts to those who would drop DVD service, he would have moved that segment over to the new model. Then he could have gone to the "light user" DVD consumers and suggested that instead of getting a new DVD any time they wanted it, they would get one once a month, say, for the same price. If they wanted the instant service their prices would go up. That would shift another bunch to at least a point of lower DVD usage. Then when these segments started to realize that all-streaming wasn't so bad, he could do the big price increase for the mainstream buyer. The point is that in trying to force customers to move faster than many of them were prepared to, Hastings exposed his company to a strategic miscue.

Hail Mary: The Core Business Is Under Immediate Threat and It Sure Feels Like a Crisis

This is a situation you don't ever want to be in. The core business is under immediate market share and margin threat, there's no silver bullet in the pipeline, and you have to make a choice—fast—about where you are going to focus. Imagine the situation at Nokia: a deep recession dampening demand for its products across the line, losses in some of its core businesses, failure to adequately penetrate emerging growth markets, leadership instability, and a collapsing share price. Oh, sorry, I'm not talking about the Nokia of 2011. I'm talking about the Nokia of the late 1980s, when the embattled company was so down on its luck that its leaders took the humiliating step of shopping the company to Swedish rival Ericsson, only to be turned down.

Speaking to me some years later, Matti Alahuhta, one of the executive team members who participated in what eventually became a spectacular turnaround, said, "You know, back then it was almost easy. We had no other choice." The company decided to pin its hopes to its nascent telecommunications business, depending on assets from previous investments in computerization and communication technologies and the acquisition of the previous state-owned telecom monopolies. It shed everything else. Rubber boots, cable manufacturing, the other industrial businesses, the TV business—gone, gone, and gone. This is the nature of disengagement when the core business is on the brink of becoming irrelevant.

But of course, you could write a similar story about Nokia today, a company that I've studied, worked with, and watched for many years. Like many people, I was very admiring when I first started interacting with it in 2000: the company's success was absolutely amazing, as it had grown with the mobile handset category in a rather spectacular manner for some time. But as I began to spend more time with the company, first in its Choices program for the Nokia Ventures Organization, and later on in a number of its management programs, I began to be concerned. Its venturing process, which I had long held up as a fantastic example (and studied, with results published in several academic articles), seemed to be losing senior executive support.[10] The appointment of a new CEO with more of a numbers orientation and less of a product orientation resulted in the loss of many talented people. And although it was growing like gangbusters in places such as India and China, the company was nowhere in the United States, despite years of strategy statements that said the United States was a core target market for it.

As a veteran Nokia watcher and industry expert said to me, "Their biggest problem is complacency." Leaning back over his desk, and perfectly mimicking the body language of a fair number of Nokia leaders at the time, he knitted his hands together and said, "In fact, they are actually complacent about their attitude toward complacency." At the time, I laughed. I laughed again when working with the company in 2001. There I was in a frozen hotel in Oulu, Finland, with a bunch of Nokia engineers. The subject of the newly released iPod came up. The reaction was entirely dismissive. "That?" they said. "It's just a hard drive built on older technology in a fancy case." I stopped working actively with the company around 2006, but by this time warning bells were ringing every time I learned afresh about management decisions that were being made.

I was dismayed to receive this e-mail from a colleague, who had worked on a number of research projects involving Nokia, dated January 2007:

> *Rita,*
>
> *Today I had a very interesting meeting at Nokia. I didn't get to meet the head of the New Business Group because he had to go out of town last minute but met his strategy director. Since*

they had a lot of personnel change (CEO as well as the head of what was NVO) they have reinvented their new business development once again. They went completely away from venturing and now view what was the NVO as a business group of its own that should show revenue AND growth. They have abandoned pretty much all early stage activities (e.g. divesting Innovent last August) and try to gain access to different business areas in the form of what they call projects or business lines . . . In my view they are setting themselves up for major failure and even worse many in the organization are aware of that (the Strategy Director was talking about how everything is dependent on the people in some key positions).

Well, by this time, dear reader, you know where this is heading. My colleague and I had a phone conversation later, in which we decided for teaching purposes to drop Nokia as an exemplary innovator. That was in 2007. Now it is 2012, and the company is once again staring at the brink.

Stephen Elop, the CEO that Nokia brought over from the Office business at Microsoft, faced almost exactly the same challenge that the company leaders of the late 1980s faced. What should be jettisoned so that the company could move onto its next growth trajectory? I first met Stephen when he was with Microsoft, running its core $19 billion Office franchise. He was interested in sharing points of view on strategy, growth, the right size for the business, how to handle freeing up resources from the core franchise to go after new areas, how they had blundered in a few key places—in short, a lot of the things that I thought would be very helpful for the software giant to think about.

So what was Elop's big disengagement decision at Nokia? To drop development of Nokia's operating system, MeeGo, and instead adopt Microsoft's Windows 7 software. The decision was not arrived at lightly: MeeGo had been widely talked about as the company's answer to Android and Apple smartphones and was to play a part in saving the company. A review of the product conducted by Elop and chief development officer Kai Oistämö, in which they interviewed twenty people deeply involved with the MeeGo project, resulted in a sad, stunning conclusion. At the best rate of progress, the company would introduce only three MeeGo-powered handsets before 2014, far too late to address the crisis besetting Nokia's core business.[11] Elop made the decision to stop the development effort and instead repurpose the talent who had been working on the doomed operating system to more future-oriented projects. Using Apple's operating system was out of the question. Working with Google's Android operating system would fail to position Nokia for leadership (and provide competition for Nokia's Navteq unit). That left Microsoft. Although the software company's share in the smartphone market in the United States was extremely small, reviews of its operating system were favorable. More important, Microsoft has strong alliances with corporations and distribution partners that could help Nokia gain traction in its long-lusted-after American markets.

The strategy now comes in three parts: First, get back in the game in smartphones using the Microsoft software to move more quickly than Nokia could have with its own software. Next, make sure the company has an emerging market presence. And, in the medium term, as a *BusinessWeek* article describes,

Elop's third priority has been dubbed New Disruptions. It's a fully sanctioned skunkworks, with teams in Helsinki and Silicon Valley, staffed by top technical talent from the discontinued Symbian and MeeGo efforts, especially MeeGo. That initiative began when Nokia hired a crew of inventive open source evangelists in 2009 with orders to dream up entirely new devices. A few months later they were reassigned to develop a replacement for Symbian. The goal, as Elop told a group of engineers in Berlin on Feb. 29, is once again to "find that next big thing that blows away Apple, Android, and everything we're doing with Microsoft right now and makes it irrelevant—all of it. So go for it, without having to worry about saving Nokia's rear end in the next 12 months. I've taken off the handcuffs."[12]

Will it work? I don't know. By the time a company is wrestling with this form of disengagement, there are many things that can go wrong, and Nokia has lost a lot of time. On the other hand, just as the company realized in an earlier era, there was very little choice. By October of 2011, the first smartphones resulting from the alliance were on the market to critical acclaim, with headlines blaring "Nokia Gets Back in the Game." We shall see what the next chapter brings.

Garage Sale: The Business Has Value, but It Isn't for Us Anymore

Some businesses without a particular advantage still have good growth or cash-flow potential, but not with the overhead cost structure or margins that the parent company is used to. The way pharmaceutical companies treat off-patent drugs reflects this dilemma—whereas a generics drug business may look unattractive to an organization such as Merck or Novartis, it looks brilliantly attractive to low-cost global competitor Teva. Similarly, the phone directory business looked like a route to commodity hell to Verizon, but was eagerly snapped up by two private equity firms, attracted by the consistent cash flows the business threw off.

Under Ivan Seidenberg, Verizon's long-time CEO, the company pursued an aggressive strategy of moving out of slow-growth former core businesses such as landlines and into more competitive and risky, but faster-growth, areas including wireless and data services. Prodded to some extent by my Columbia Business School colleague Bruce Greenwald, as early as 2001, Seidenberg was anticipating the fading of existing advantages, expecting annual revenues over $100 billion, with 35 percent coming from wireless and 20 percent from data.[13] He also anticipated that traditional voice revenues would represent only about 35 percent of the total book of business, down from 60 percent. Since then, the company has shed slow-growth units (even those with solid cash flows), such as phone directories.[14] In their place—and using the cash these spun-off businesses yielded—Verizon has made massive investments in such new areas as fiber optic service technology to enable it to compete with cable companies in offering television and internet services. Seidenberg did what many companies fail to do: make aggressive investments in the company's future while the core business was still generating substantial cash.

One of the stiffest challenges of exiting the core business and repositioning the company in growth spaces is convincing the investment community that this is the right thing to do. Verizon's stock was battered for years as it poured money into broadband offerings. Beginning in 2007, however, articles with titles such as "Verizon's Big TV Bet Pays Off" started to appear. And in early 2009, an article in *Barron's* about Verizon began like this: "In times that are anything but normal, it pays to invest in a company that delivers reliable, business-as-usual results, keeps its focus on avenues of growth and holds the promise of market-beating returns. Verizon Communications, the New York-based telecommunications giant, fits the bill nicely."[15]

The vindication must have been gratifying for Verizon, given the boldness of the company's moves out of its former core business.

Fire Sale: A Garage Sale in a Hurry

One of the most frustrating things about the temporary-advantage phenomenon for a management educator is that no sooner do you find a great example of a company that is doing something really interesting, strategically, than that company falls victim to the stings of eroding advantage. The later poor performance then completely discredits the interesting idea they began with. That's a bit the way I feel about Mexican cement producer CEMEX. Not that I'm alone—many management researchers have written admiringly of the plucky regional firm that through innovation, clever use of digital technologies, and aggressive M&A activity rose to become a global player and is today the world's third-largest cement company.

Unfortunately, some poorly timed acquisitions and the global construction slowdown have created a real black eye for CEMEX, with a near bankruptcy in 2009 and losses in the third quarter of 2011 alone totaling $821.7 million.[16] With the core business under threat, CEMEX proceeded with a substantial disengagement of so-called noncore assets, to the tune of $1 billion's worth by the end of 2012, to reduce debt and meet financing covenants. Lorenzo Zambrano, CEMEX's CEO, has thrown down the gauntlet for businesses wishing to remain within the corporate parent's purview: earn 10 percent return on capital, or you are on the block. On the list are quarries, assets held in joint ventures, real estate, and other idle assets that don't produce earnings before interest, taxes, depreciation, and amortization by the end of the year.[17]

Unlike the more modulated asset disposals of the previous category, such fire sales are often made under significant duress as investors and analysts, armed with metaphorical pitchforks, put pressure on management to stem the losses, focus, and create a compelling story for why the firm is going to get out of its rut. As my friend and colleague Harry Korine has often pointed out, activist investors can sometimes provide a pivotal push to a management team that is reluctant to make some tough choices in this regard.

Run-off: A Declining Technology or Capability, but Someone Still Wants It

Even when something is in an end-of-life stage, there are often important constituents who are still depending on it. A firm at that point has to figure out some way of shrinking the business to the right size while providing appropriate support to the customers and other stakeholders who may be left behind. Often, these are niche customers who are relatively price insensitive and have a deep need.

Privately held GDCA (formerly GD California) provides a fascinating example of a company that benefits from product obsolescence by allowing client firms to sunset older technologies without abandoning commitments to key customers. When mainstream manufacturers of computer equipment (such as boards) respond to technological improvements and end-of-product-life decisions by getting rid of older equipment and filling their factories with shiny new machines, they create enormous problems for manufacturers of precision medical, military, and industrial equipment who have embedded the boards in their own products. When the components are changed, this can necessitate a product redesign on their part, which in turn can trigger the need for a renewed round of qualifications and a certification that the equipment will work properly. With end-of-life situations occurring with greater frequency, the previous solution of simply buying up enough of the old boards to meet expected demand was proving expensive and unwieldy.

Into this breach stepped GDCA, which counterintuitively went into the business of manufacturing obsolete board designs to guarantee the downstream customers that they could continue to buy the exact boards embedded in their designs. Its Availability Assurance Program is essentially an insurance policy against component obsolescence and the resulting problem for customers. Subscribers turn to GDCA when the original manufacturer decides to discontinue making a board. The company then transfers the technology from the original manufacturer to its own engineering group, stores spares, produces more units if necessary, provides repairs, and, when the customer eventually decides it is ready to move on, closes the program. As of 2003, subscriptions were $10,500 per event, plus $3,000 annual maintenance per board.[18] It is worth noting that GDCA has also benefited from the declining category by developing an innovative business model—insurance, rather than simply relying on manufacturing.

A consideration for many technology companies in this "shrink to the right size" strategy is that they often risk losing valuable technology capabilities when the business in which they were developed is discontinued. To address that issue, companies often develop a special business unit just to focus on keeping those capabilities alive. Telecommunications manufacturer Avaya, for example, maintains what is called a "custom engineering" unit, which basically keeps capabilities on the shelf but which can reinvigorate them when they seem relevant once more to a customer's problem or retire them when the customer no longer needs support. Mohamad Ali, Avaya's former head of strategy, explained the mechanism the company uses for "keeping certain capabilities alive." After early adopters have agreed to purchase a given solution, he said, "You can't just kill it and leave your customers in the lurch."

He gave an example of a product the company had developed for Citibank in Japan, developing what it terms a "thin call" solution in which customers can interact with a teller remotely, using a phone and a video feed to allow the teller to interact with a customer who could be hundreds of miles away. As he put it, "Let's say we decide to kill thin call. Citibank isn't going to like it if we abandon them. So we put it in the custom engineering group. As long as Citibank is a customer, we'll continue to support it." The custom engineering group is also a place in which Avaya keeps people and know-how accessible, even if it doesn't draw on them for an immediate product. This illustrates two principles for effective disengagement: (1) that you don't lose key capabilities because a business ends, and (2) that stakeholders who are adversely affected by your decision to stop doing something are made whole.

Last Man Standing

One strategy for disengagement is to effectively lead the market down by prompting consolidation of a declining industry and remaining as one of its leading suppliers. The strategic logic here is that a business in decline requires relatively low investments, costs are sunk, and, to the extent that you aren't facing competitors in survival mode, cash flows can actually be quite good even if volumes are going down. Of course, for this strategy to work, not all players in the business can pursue it successfully: some will have to be prompted to exit. The process can be helped along by one competitor that can operate with extreme efficiency, cutting costs to the point at which others drop out. Another way of reducing excess capacity is to reduce it yourself by buying other companies' assets, taking over their production capacity, forming joint ventures that take out capacity, or acting as an outsourced partner. There is also, for the strong of constitution, the option of aggressively investing in the declining category, making it far less attractive for competitors to remain. This was the strategy quite successfully pursued by Jon Huntsman, Sr. of Huntsman Chemicals in consolidating various industries, such as that for textile dyes and the chemicals used to create "clamshell" containers for fast-food chains.

Such a strategy is not without its risks, of course, because the behavior of competitors and likely future pricing in an industry are hard to anticipate. An interesting sector that illustrates this beautifully is the global steel business. No one would accuse Lakshmi Mittal, the CEO of ArcelorMittal, as lacking in confidence or vision. Following the mantra "Boldness changes everything," Mittal has engineered dozens of sometimes controversial mergers. The one that brought him attention on the world stage for the first time was when his Indian firm, which had grown to a substantial size, made a play for the French steelmaker Arcelor in 2006. The French were dismissive (the stocks proposed to fund the deal were referred to as "monkey money"), and Europeans in general were alarmed that a firm from an emerging economy could muster the strength to take over a European icon.[19]

Mittal prevailed, the acquisition of Arcelor being just one more milestone in the realization of a twenty-year vision to prompt consolidation of the global steel business with the goal of attaining a leadership position in this industry where there are few remaining competitive advantages other than cost. Unfortunately for Mittal, years of effort have not yielded the desired cost efficiencies or consolidation benefits, and in the summer of 2010 ArcelorMittal announced that it intended to spin off its stainless-steel business. The situation reflects the classic difficulty of trying to lead in a declining arena. As one observer (a Nordic-based analyst who declined to be named) remarked, "It would benefit the sector if capacity were cut, but no one wants to volunteer. I tend to think nothing will happen."

So, there we have the principles of healthy disengagement. First, identify the warning signs. Often, these are qualitative leading indicators rather than quantitative lagging ones. Next, create a way for the import of the numbers to be recognized. Then, once the decision has been made, determine the situation you are in and design the disengagement strategy that makes the most sense.

As you will have seen by now, conventional budgeting and planning processes are unlikely to be of much help in a transient-advantage context. The decision to exit a business and to implement that exit effectively requires the ability to break through budget logjams and effectively move resources to other places. In the next chapter, we'll look in more depth at how what I call "deft" organizations use their resources to increase responsiveness and flexibility as they move from advantage to advantage.

Note: For a discussion of how to conduct a value-capturing disengagement review, see chapter 8 of *Discovery-Driven Growth*.

4

Using Resource Allocation to Promote Deftness

If you want to shape the way an organization behaves, an extraordinarily robust conclusion from academic research is that the resource allocation process is key.[1] Firms built to thrive under transient-advantage conditions handle resources differently from firms designed for exploitation. In an exploitation-oriented firm, reliable performance, scale, and replication of processes from one place to another make a lot of sense because you can operate more efficiently and gain the benefits of scale. Resources, therefore, are directed to support these goals, and changing these resource flows is painful and difficult. A transient-advantage-oriented firm, on the other hand, allocates resources to promote what I call deftness—the ability to reconfigure and change processes with a certain amount of ease, quickly.

In a typical firm, resources are controlled by powerful existing businesses, and the powerful people are those who dominated the last-generation competitive advantage. That means that new opportunities are often force-fit into an existing structure, if they survive at all. In a transient-advantage firm, resources are directed by a governance mechanism that is separate from any given business unit. Moreover, structures that suit the new opportunities are created. In a typical firm, every effort is made to squeeze as much operating margin out of existing assets as possible. In a transient-advantage firm, people realize that the competitive life of an asset may be different from its accounting life, and move to retire those that are no longer competitive before they desperately have to. Such firms realize that in contrast to the concept of "terminal value" from net present value (NPV)–oriented calculations, what one has instead is "asset debt"—the investment necessary to keep all assets at competitive best in class. In a typical firm, allocations of resources for growth (say) are handled with a capital budgeting mind-set, in which big black hole–type investments are made in the hopes of a huge payback. In a transient-advantage-oriented firm, instead, resources are managed with extreme parsimony, only being invested after a concept is proven. Finally, in a typical firm, ownership of assets is seen as critical because in the past owning assets created entry barriers. Firms adept at managing transient advantage recognize instead that today, access to assets, rather than ownership, provides flexibility and scalability without having to commit to a particular path and that the ready ability to access assets eliminates the advantage of actually owning them, in many cases. Table 4-1 sums up these differences.

TABLE 4-1

The new strategy playbook: resources and organization

From	To
Resources held hostage in business units	Resources under a central governance mechanism
Squeezing opportunities into the existing structure	Organizing around opportunities
Attempts to extend the useful life of assets for as long as possible	Aggressive and proactive retirement of competitively obsolete assets
Terminal value	Asset debt
Capital budgeting mind-set	Real options mind-set—variable costs, flexible investments
Investment-intensive strategic initiatives	Parsimony, parsimony, parsimony
Ownership is key	Access is key
Build it yourself	Leverage external resources

The Resources as Hostage Problem

As I pointed out in chapters 2 and 3, a core implication of transient advantage is that what is good for a particular business may not be good for the organization as a whole. In a traditional company, people who had lots of assets and staff reporting to them were the important people in the company. This idea was reinforced by systems such as the Hay Group's point allocation, in which more pay and power were assumed to go to those managers with bigger operations. Indeed, just recently I was chatting with the head of talent development for a major publishing firm, who believes that this way of rating people is their single biggest obstacle to becoming a more nimble competitor. The bigger-is-better mind-set is deadly in an environment in which advantages come and go. If people feel their authority, power base, and other rewards will be diminished if they move assets or people out of an existing advantage, they will fight tooth and nail to preserve the status quo.

Sony provides a clear cautionary tale. It yielded dominance in portable music to Apple. It ceded leadership in entire display technologies, such as plasma and LED, to other firms. It has no presence in many of today's most exciting technologies, such as touchscreen computing devices. As an insider told me, "Sony was trapped by its own competitive advantages. They wanted to protect their technologies. When customers would ask [former CEO] Idei why the company didn't make plasma or high definition televisions, he would say to them that Trinitron is superior technology." Superior, no matter what the customers said they wanted. Indeed, as far back as 2003, observers were already pointing out the dangers of the "civil war" inside Sony, as no one mediated the difference in objectives between the content divisions and the hardware divisions of the company.[2]

Instead of allowing resources to be allocated at the level of individual businesses, a critical condition for competing in transient-advantage situations is to have a governance process for controlling resources that is not under the control of business unit leaders. Recall Sanjay Purohit at Infosys being asked to take resources back that were underemployed—remarkable! Wresting control from powerful people is not always easy, but it is absolutely essential if one is to avoid the organization's interests being subsumed by what is good for an individual leader. In moving Wolters Kluwer from existing business models to digital ones, Nancy McKinstry used control over the capital allocation process as one of her key levers. Indeed, when I asked her what advice she would give to other CEOs faced with such a massive transformation in their business, she said, "My advice to other CEOs is to focus on capital allocation."

Run Nonnegotiable Legacy Assets for Efficiency

Just as you need to reconfigure existing structures to go after new opportunities, so too you need to deal with the assets tied up with those existing structures. In many cases, they are still important to your organization, but they are no longer growth opportunities. The watchword here is to extract as many resources as you can from running these activities, because they no longer represent opportunity. Further, they can become obstacles to creating a deft organization because they tend to preserve processes that were designed to support a now-commoditizing business. Deconstructing reward systems, processes, legacy programs, structures, networks, and other elements used to deliver to an old advantage is not going to happen by accident and calls for real leadership. At IBM, for instance, stopping projects such as OS2 and exiting the PC business were both moves that freed up resources, time, and attention to be able to focus on opportunities.

The eroding differentiation of legacy assets can sneak up on you if you aren't strategically alert. In past work, I've commented on the fact that what was once exciting and sexy about a product, service, or other offering that companies provide eventually becomes a commoditized nonnegotiable attribute.[3] That means that customers expect something similar from all providers. The dilemma is that these things are often highly expensive table stakes. Not offering them to customers enrages them, but offering them, even offering them exceptionally well, does nothing for you competitively. Network reliability in your cable service, clean beds in hotel rooms, car ignitions that routinely start, restaurants that deliver what you ordered, accurate bills—all these things are hard to do. Because you have to do them but they don't add to margin or gain you market share, the mantra for delivering them has to be to focus on cost savings. The slide from exciting to nonnegotiable means you need to change how you run the assets that deliver expensive nonnegotiable attributes.

This may be the time to bring in a rock-ribbed exploitation expert to wring every last bit of productivity out of existing assets. This is what happened at Apple when Steve Jobs returned to run the company in 1997 and astonished everybody by moving quickly to instill world-class operating capabilities in the areas of manufacturing, finance, and back office functions.[4]

There are a number of ways in which nondifferentiating activities can be made more economical. One is to centralize them under a shared-services model to end duplication of things being done in many places. Another is to create absolutely standardized processes rather than continue to support dozens of idiosyncratically designed ways of working. Remember, the activity or thing in question is not delivering a competitive advantage, so it really can't justify being highly customized—it's common in the industry. Simplification—such as eliminating handovers, automating portions, or making some of a process user generated—is a further source of cost savings. And of course outsourcing makes sense as well, particularly if the activity is not part of your competitive secret sauce. For instance, CAT Telecom and TOT Plc, two telecom operators in Thailand, plan to merge their wireless 3G networks.[5] Running a network no longer offers competitive advantage, so why not share the costs of the nonnegotiable offer and compete on the basis of services? Giant telecom services provider Ericsson has capitalized on this idea, running networks for clients and offering technologies that it does not see as differentiating for itself.

Proactively Retire Assets That Are No Longer at the Competitive Edge

Eventually, with most legacy assets, there comes a time when you have to make the decision to retire them altogether. To illustrate this process, let's have a look at what Frank Modruson, the chief information officer (CIO) of consultancy Accenture, has done over a more than ten-year period of systematically replacing obsolete assets. Modruson doesn't look like a revolutionary—he's a calm, thoughtful guy who considers carefully what he's about to say before he says it. But the change he led at Accenture's IT organization was quietly revolutionary. As he describes it, the legacy systems in place in most organizations are like "concrete shoes," the exact opposite of the deft structures that are needed to cope with transient advantages.

Like any other business asset, information systems depreciate. Over time, they eventually become competitively obsolete. The problem is that because vital corporate information resides in these systems, replacing and upgrading them is disruptive and expensive. Moreover, unlike physical assets such as plant and equipment, it can be hard to measure the point at which an IT system is no longer at a competitive standard. The consequence is that IT systems are typically repaired piecemeal, patched, and kept in use. CIOs often are not allocated the resources they need to replace, rather than patch, their systems. Although this doesn't look dangerous in the near term, keeping legacy systems running is a major barrier to the reconfiguration that companies need to do to gain deftness, because legacy systems reinforce legacy structures and operations.

We're talking at the moment about computer systems, but you can think about this logic for any class of legacy assets. Have a look at figure 4-1. It shows the decade-by-decade evolution of

FIGURE 4-1

Evolving technology regimes in information technology

	1960s				2010s
Computer infrastructure	Mainframes	Minicomputers	AS/400	PCs and laptops	PDA phones
Computer platform	1/Company	1/Location	1/Deck	1/Person	Ubiquitous
Networking	Tapes and disks	Hard-wired	Individual corporate networks	LANs, internet	WANs, wireless
Computer languages	Assembly language and COBOL	Assembly language and COBOL	FORTRAN, PL, Pascal	Visual Basic, Perl, JavaScript, C	Web
Data	VSAM	Information management systems	Relational databases	World Wide Web	Cloud
Telephony	Few; calls through switchboards	PBX office	First cell phones appear	Cell phones proliferate	VoIP; corporate voice mail disappears

Source: Copyright © 2010 Accenture.

information technologies from the 1960s through the present. In the 1960s, there were mainframes, single computing platforms per company, and no linked networks (people shared information by sharing things such as tapes and disks); Assembly and COBOL were the favored languages; data was stored in Virtual Storage Access Memory files (an old IBM standard); and telephony actually used switchboards. Over the years, the problems these technologies addressed were increasingly solved by newer, cheaper, different ways of operating. So, for instance, today consumer technologies such as personal digital assistants (PDAs) and smartphones have taken over many computing chores that once required a mainframe to tackle. The same logic applies to changes in other technologies. Since 1980, new technologies such as radio frequency identification (RFID), LED and LCD lights, twenty-four-hour ATMs, DNA testing, magnetic resonance imaging machines, heart stents, genetically modified foods, and biofuels have all offered advantages over the technologies that came before, making previous solutions obsolete.

Here's the problem: because upgrading legacy assets is expensive, there is a strong temptation among many firms to keep them running as long as possible. The result is often a bewildering patchwork of technologies that are inefficient, hard to change, and rigid. In the case of IT, it's not unusual for a CIO to be simultaneously trying to figure out how to integrate iPhones, unified communications solutions, and cloud computing approaches at the same time he or she is praying that the company's last remaining COBOL programmers don't retire and take the secrets of how certain systems work with them. It is as if Milliken & Company (the textile producer we met in chapter 2) were to try to run its business of today with the equipment it operated in the 1960s!

The consequences of "patching, patching, patching" are predictable. The organization is left with a complicated IT infrastructure that is increasingly expensive to maintain and increasingly unresponsive to the needs of the business. Technology ceases to be an enabler and becomes an inhibitor. The concept is clear in IT, but relevant to other classes of assets as well.

At Accenture, Modruson and then-CEO William (Bill) D. Green decided that if the organization aspired to excellence, it would need world-class IT infrastructure. This would require taking on the daunting task of proactively retiring older IT assets. Figure 4-2 shows what Accenture is working with today. Notice how the technologies of the 1960s, the 1970s, and the 1980s have been left behind, and the company is instead focusing on having only more current assets in place. The guiding mantra Frank adopted was that anything implemented before 2000 should be eliminated. Ask yourself—if you were to make a similar chart for the assets, processes, and technologies in place in your organization, how much would it resemble figure 4-1? Figure 4-2?

Accenture's IT journey began with the establishment of the company as a separate, publicly traded company in 2000. The company had 2,100 applications (600 global and 1,500 local). This resulted in, among other things, different views of the same data, because different systems produced different views of the same information. This created significant challenges for making timely and accurate decisions.

Modruson recently summarized the results of the company's proactive retirement of legacy assets for me: "Today, the 600 global applications have been reduced to 247, and the 1,500 local applications have been replaced by only 242. The oldest application Accenture is still running dates from 1999, and it is slated for retirement in 2012." But does all this proactive replacement of legacy assets really make a competitive difference? Absolutely. At Accenture, the percentage of revenue allocated to IT has been reduced to below industry standards, even as the company has more than tripled in size in terms of number of employees.

FIGURE 4-2

Leaving the past behind

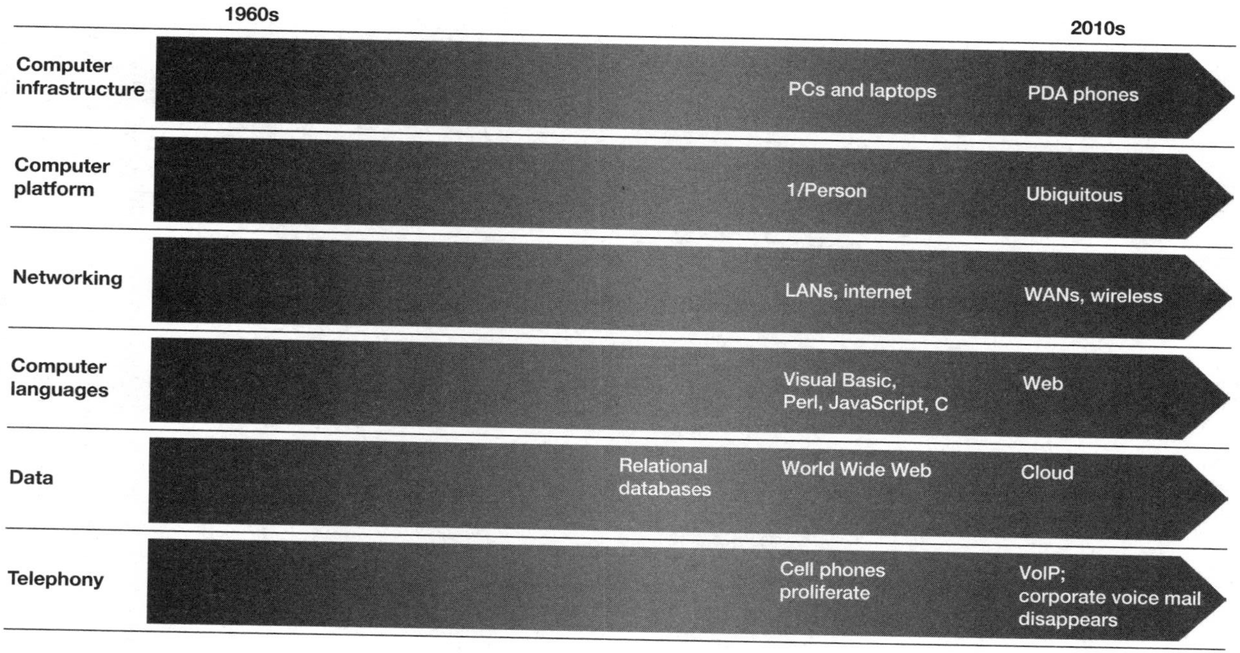
1960s
2010s
Computer infrastructure
PCs and laptops
PDA phones
Computer platform
1/Person
Ubiquitous
Networking
LANs, internet
WANs, wireless
Computer languages
Visual Basic, Perl, JavaScript, C
Web
Data
Relational databases
World Wide Web
Cloud
Telephony
Cell phones proliferate
VoIP; corporate voice mail disappears

Source: Copyright © 2010 Accenture.

Moreover, the company has enhanced its ability to move quickly because the newer systems are designed to support today's strategy, not yesterday's. That is a huge gain in deftness.

Freeing the Hostages: How Accenture Did It

I've mentioned before that it is often deadly for companies when resources are held hostage within business units. One needs to be able to wrestle control away from vested interests. At Accenture, the mechanism used was to establish an IT steering committee composed of the COOs and CEOs of the business units. Modruson established a ground rule that only the most senior people in each business unit could attend the meetings. At one point, a VP needed to beg off and asked if he could send a surrogate. "Nope," said Modruson, "but you can send your boss, if he'll come." Astonishingly, the more-senior guy did show up to attend the meeting, offering a valuable senior-level perspective to the deliberations. As Modruson explained to me, any dilution of the importance of the senior-level steering committee would have crippled their ability to govern in the face of politics and demands from the businesses to get their individual needs met.

One of Modruson's more difficult meetings took place when the IT steering committee decided not to fund a couple of his own boss's pet projects. "What," the senior guy said, "my projects fell below the cutoff? Isn't there any way to get the funding for them restored?" "Sure," said Frank. "If we allocate more funding, the projects that are below the line today might find themselves above it." Eventually, the budget in that instance was increased, but not just for the boss's pet project—for all the projects in the pipeline with that priority level. The integrity of the governance and alignment system was absolutely critical to Accenture's ability to reallocate resources.

The "cutoff" rules were driven by a number of design principles specific to IT, but the process of making such decisions is applicable to any outdated asset. In the case of Accenture, the company valued consolidation, centralization, standardization, reducing the number of applications, and creating a single instance of any given piece of data. Just as we saw with Infosys in an earlier chapter, having one version of the truth allows for greater transparency, simplicity, and far fewer time-consuming negotiations about what is really going on. Getting work done becomes easier. As Modruson told me, "We don't have those tedious and time-consuming conversations any more. There is one financial system for all of Accenture. One time and expense system. One HR system. What ends up happening is two wonderful things. The cost to run systems goes down because you have less of them. More importantly, the quality of the information goes up." A major benefit for the IT group is that by giving all of Accenture's people access to core information, each business unit can address its own information needs without turning to the IT staff, which helps it to be more productive and lessens the drain on the IT staff.

Contrast this with the experience of another multinational firm that I won't name because it is just too embarrassing. Whenever the CEO had a meeting with another CEO, it took staffers up to four *days* to pull together information about all the company's relationships with that firm. The data were hidden in various systems, spreadsheets, and even people's heads. At Accenture, Modruson told me, this task would be a trivial exercise taking just minutes. Now consider the benefit to a firm like Accenture, and the commensurate disadvantage of the other firm in a context in which advantages are temporary.

The Concept of Asset Debt

Modruson coined the phrase "technology debt." What this means is that keeping technology in a fit state to support a company's competitiveness requires continual investment and a willingness to leave older assets behind. I would extend that more broadly to the concept of any asset that a firm might possess. Everybody knows that without maintenance, bridges, roads and tunnels, and other assets eventually break down. The important point is that the competitive life of an asset may be different (and usually shorter) than its accounting life. You can think of setting aside resources for investment in revitalizing your assets as an obligation similar to your company's pension fund or other obligations. This thinking flies in the face of conventional NPV-based logic, however, in which even at the end of their useful lives assets are considered to have a terminal value. There is usually no such thing—instead, a company needs to be thinking of continually investing to refresh older assets.

Today, Accenture is continuing its pattern of investments. Major projects in the second half of the decade include applications rationalization, replacing the internal network, rationalizing its data center, and investing in data center virtualization. The network transformation program, for instance, let Accenture set up a cost-effective videoconferencing network. Aside from making collaboration far easier, it's also had a positive second-order effect of diminishing the amount of travel its consultants need to engage in.

Configure the Organization to the Opportunity, Not the Other Way Around

Just as shifting economic resources, such as budgets, is a key lever for increasing an organization's level of deftness, so too is shifting power structures within the organization. We already saw, in chapter 2, how organizations such as Infosys proactively change their structures in order to unleash growth potential, arguing that allowing an existing structure to remain in place for too long creates inertia and results in an organization that is maladapted to the opportunities it finds. As Brad Anderson, former CEO of Best Buy, said in a session at the World Economic Forum meetings in 2009, "Organizations have habits. And they will cling to their habits at the expense sometimes of their own survival." Breaking those habits often requires a structural solution.

One clear indicator that structure is getting in the way is when opportunities seem to fall between the cracks. I had first-hand experience observing this at DuPont, in a major project designed to, as former CEO Chad Holiday said, "get paid for what we know, what came to be called the 'knowledge intensive growth program.'"[6] DuPont historically relied on business models in which it gave away its knowledge in the form of consulting or advice in order to sell products. Holiday's concept was that the firm should instead start getting paid for the value it created for customers, even if that value came from a service rather than a material. This was a sea-change for the two-hundred-year-old company.

At the time, DuPont was structured into strategic business units (SBUs), with each business unit leader responsible for that unit's own assets, sales, marketing, and so on. The "aha" moment came when a team consisting of DuPont's KIU director, Bob Cooper, and a few of us from academia, did an analysis of specific growth opportunities. Almost all of these fell outside the domain of any SBU. The SBU heads had little incentive to cooperate with one another or to promote new business models. To address this issue, DuPont had to massively reconfigure the company. The solution it hit on was to create what it called "growth platforms." Each platform was given a specific broad domain that it could pursue, regardless of where the assets and people happened to be located within a particular business. Ellen Kullman was put in charge of the "Safety and Protection" platform, charged with going after unfamiliar business models that cut across former SBU territories. It was scary at first. "I spend a lot of time talking people off of ledges," she told me at the time of the change. Her results were outstanding. From 2004 to 2008, the Safety and Protection Division posted record revenue gains of 64 percent and led to her appointment as the storied firm's CEO.[7]

Approach Resources with an Entrepreneurial Mind-Set: Options-Oriented Investments

Established organizations tend to put far too much money behind new ideas, treating them as though they know exactly what will happen, even though they are highly uncertain. One of the unfortunate consequences is that when things don't go as planned, there is an overwhelming tendency to persist, because the sunk costs look frightening to write off. This in turn often leads to painful and expensive flops, from massive product failures such as the Iridium project to disastrous acquisitions, such as the $850 million AOL basically wasted purchasing social networking site Bebo. A more effective approach in uncertain environments is to allow resources to be invested only when uncertainty is reduced, a core principle of options reasoning.

The companies led by entrepreneurs are often forced, by dint of simply not having a lot of resources, to operate in a lean, parsimonious way. To cite MacMillan, "They spend their imaginations before they spend money." As a consequence, they gain deftness in the form of flexibility, few sunk costs, speed, and accelerated learning. This is consistent with the "options orientation" we discussed when we were looking at how the growth outliers get into and out of businesses. There are major lessons to be gained for resource allocation in large organizations from examining how they leverage their assets and resources. Two rich examples are TerraCycle and Under Armour.

TerraCycle got its start in 2001 when Tom Szaky and Jon Beyer, both Princeton freshmen, became interested in the role that composting might play in the then-emerging market for organic products. According to company lore, the actual inspiration was some Canadian friends' success at using feces from red worms as fertilizer for a few home-grown marijuana plants.[8] Szaky and Beyer conceived of a business that would use leftover food and other biodegradable waste as worm food, then use the worm excrement (to attract PR, they always refer to it as "worm poop") to make high-quality organic fertilizer. They lost a business plan competition, but started the business anyway.

It was a classic low-budget start-up. They collected their raw material input in the form of biodegradable leftovers and empty bottles from Princeton University's own dining halls. They scavenged furniture from students who left it behind at term's end. Their initial investment in the business was about $20,000 for the conversion equipment, supplemented by angel investors. The business was set up in a down-at-the-heels part of Trenton, New Jersey. Initially, they reached out to green websites dedicated to the ecologically minded. Rather than use paid advertising, they developed an amazingly effective process for generating free publicity (which today they calculate to be worth about $52 million, including a National Geographic TV show, *Garbage Moguls*). Eventually the company expanded to offer its organic fertilizer to huge retailers such as Walmart and Home Depot. In 2007, a big incumbent firm, Scotts Miracle-Gro (a $2.7-billion-revenue company) decided that $1.4-million-revenue TerraCycle was a threat and slapped a 173-page lawsuit against the tiny company.[9] The David-versus-Goliath struggle created a media free-for-all and put TerraCycle on the map. The lawsuit was eventually settled, but the publicity was priceless.[10]

In true options fashion, TerraCycle keeps its resource commitments fluid. As Szaky noted in a book he wrote about the business: "[I]t would have been impossible to predict or plan how to develop TerraCycle so that it would make it to the place it stands today. The trick was to be ever vigilant in seeking opportunities and to be ready to jump on them if they felt right inside and consistent with our core mission, even before they could be well thought out."[11] The company has stuck to its broad theme of supporting green business, but has extended its operations into a wide variety of additional arenas beyond fertilizer. Today, it is involved in so-called upscaling, in which by-products such as packaging are converted to new end products, as well as other green initiatives for large brand marketers. The company is rapidly expanding globally, with offices in far-flung places such as Brazil and a plan to become a billion-dollar enterprise in the green remediation space.

In a company geared toward transient advantage, the discipline of maintaining absolute resource parsimony is pervasive. The point is to keep investments to a rock-bottom minimum until cash-positive sales can be secured. Tom Szaky's story of TerraCycle is an example. Another is the story of Under Armour, discussed in the next section.

Parsimony, Parsimony, Parsimony

Kevin Plank was a football player for the University of Maryland in the early 1990s. He is intense, with an athlete's build and a bring-it-on-if-you-dare swagger. By the time I met him in person, in 2010, Under Armour, the clothing company he cofounded with fellow football player Jordan Lindgren, was generating close to a billion in revenue each year. The company has held its own in the face of fierce competition from the likes of Nike and Adidas, has over two thousand employees, and is continuing a pace of steady growth. And it is an outstanding example of remaining parsimonious in the use of resources.

The inspiration for Under Armour's initial product came from Plank's own athletic experience. The t-shirts athletes wore at the time were typically cotton, and during a rough practice they became soaked and, aside from being disgusting, started to get in the way. The tight, synthetic compression shorts he wore, meanwhile, stayed dry. He was inspired to find a way to make a t-shirt that would have the dryness, wicking, and comfort-enhancing properties of the synthetic shorts. Plank thus conceived of a new category of clothing, athletic performance wear, even though he didn't invent the fabric (our friends at Milliken & Company actually did a lot of that).

The start-up was a model of parsimony. Plank spent much of 1996 in his Ford Explorer, visiting locker rooms throughout the Atlantic Coast Conference. He personally spent time with players, equipment managers, and others influential in selecting gear. His authenticity as a fellow football player and ability to articulate clearly why his products were superior created a powerful point of differentiation that was simultaneously easy to communicate. "We make athletes perform better" proclaims the company website, a claim that has not varied since his original inspiration.

Plank skillfully leveraged the loyal following among college football athletes to extend to pro athletes, eventually positioning the product with very visible and respected public figures. He proved skilled at getting inexpensive but high-impact attention. For instance, following his gift of samples, Oliver Stone's movie *Any Given Sunday* featured Willie Beamen, played by Jamie Foxx, wearing an Under Armour jockstrap. The company successfully defined itself as the leading, disruptive player in the performance wear

A Meme on a Budget: Protect This House

As a *Fast Company* story reported in 2005,

[B]ecause [Plank] was thoroughly outmanned, he had to do more with less. He recruited dozens of college and pro players as his unofficial marketers. "Try it," he told them, "and if you like it, give one to the guy with the locker next to you."

For Under Armour's first TV ad in 2003, the goal was to create a spot that would live longer than its 30 seconds on the air, says Steve Battista, director of marketing. The commercial showed a football squad huddled around Eric Ogbogu, one of Plank's former teammates and a defensive end for the Dallas Cowboys. He shouted, "We must protect this house!" as if his life depended on it.

The reaction was a marketer's dream—more than 50,000 calls and e-mails from athletes, coaches, even execs. Consumers sent in stories and tapes of themselves invoking the rallying cry at games, and even at sales meetings. Protect this house! banners appeared at NFL stadiums. ESPN anchor Stuart Scott and David Letterman quoted the phrase. It became shorthand for the brand, like "Just do it."[a]

a. C. Salter, "Protect This House," *Fast Company*, August 1, 2005.

category. Today, Under Armour is a billion-dollar-plus business and maintains a strong hold on its category, although it is aware that things may change. The doors of the company's product design area are overshadowed by a sign reading "We Have Not Yet Built Our Defining Product"—a symbol of a company that is keenly aware that advantages can be transient.[12]

Access to Assets, Not Ownership of Assets

At one time, asset intensity provided many businesses with the gift of creating entry barriers. When big investments were necessary to be competitive, it was hard for newcomers to become serious rivals. That situation has changed considerably in many industries. Say I were to give you the following challenge: create an organization that could compete head-to-head with any *Fortune* 500 company, without investing in any assets that you yourself owned. Thirty years ago, this would have been a preposterous proposition. Today, it is completely feasible. Increasingly, our world is one in which one pays for access to the assets one needs, rather than having to own them outright.

Consider my challenge—how would you meet it? The process would look a lot more like making a movie, running a political campaign, or staging the Olympics than the way most organizations operate today. You might contract with an innovation firm such as Innosight or Strategyn to help flesh out the business parameters and operating model. You might use a firm such as oDesk to get programming and technical work done. For jobs that require a human touch but which are easy to describe, you could use Amazon's "Mechanical Turk" and pay by the task. Amazon can also provide you with massive amounts of computing capacity without your having to build a single server. Need specialized expertise? Guru.com has hundreds of highly qualified specialists on call in its network. InnoCentive can help you solve specific technical problems by giving you access to its network of "solvers." You can get Regus to provide you with flexible, easily changed office space. Employees? Do you really need employees when firms such as Skills Hive or Adecco can provide you with skilled people in an on-demand way? The pace of competition sheds an entirely different perspective on how organizations and the resources tied to them relate.

The reason access, rather than ownership, is increasingly attractive is that it allows firms to adjust their structures and assets quickly as competitive dynamics unfold. Indeed, we are seeing increasing evidence of CEOs attempting to do exactly this in increasingly large swaths of our economy. The necessary resources are assembled to tackle a specific task or problem, and when the work is done the organization, such as it is, is disassembled and moves on to the next task. On-demand computing capacity, offered by organizations such as Amazon, "instant" factories available on the cheap for instant utilization, and technologies that can make anyone a skilled machinist or manufacturer are here today, ready to be accessed rather than owned. What we will see, increasingly, is a core of individuals who represent the long-term interests of the organization (its leaders and long-term staff) guiding the efforts of other people whose attachment is more episodic.

You can see the trend in the data on temporary employment. Employers are relying more on temporary workers rather than full-time workers, and this does not appear to be only a factor of the recession. The *New York Times*, citing Bureau of Labor statistics data, compared the percentage of new hires who were temporary workers across three different periods of recession (table 4-2).[13]

The temporary or "disposable" organizational form is all around us, and it fits well with strategies of rapid prototyping, quickly

TABLE 4-2

Trends in temporary employment

Period of economic recovery	Share of temporary as opposed to permanently employed workers hired
1992–1993	11%
2003–2004	7%
2009–2010	26%

capitalizing on opportunities, and being willing to exit fast. In retailing, pop-up shops can mock up and test concepts without the commitment of a long-term lease. Even in manufacturing, processes that used to require casting techniques, precision tools, and years of experience to craft molds for devices can now be done quickly using digital files. An entire category of firms offering manufacturing-on-demand makes it possible to pilot and test new concepts for physical goods without the need for fixed plants and equipment. T-shirts from Threadless, manufactured goods from New Zealand–based Ponoko, self-published books from Lulu.com, and fashion design from Spreadshirt all allow small quantities of products to be created without fixed assets or significant up-front investment. Because their business model is often that no money exchanges hands until a customer actually buys a product, profitability can be built in right from the outset.

In addition, large swaths of work that can be modularized and shipped overseas are being handled in just that way. Everything from reading radiology scans to scanning legal documents is work that is finding its way to cheaper locales as companies attempt to offload the human capital tied up in doing these tasks. And, of course, outsourcing of tasks such as running call centers, managing computer networks, and handling noncore tasks for organizations is a well-established trend. The key point is that you don't need to own an asset yourself to benefit from its services. A related theme is to leverage external resources to the extent that you can, rather than trying to complete an ecosystem all by yourself. A disturbing open issue is that although increasing flexibility helps organizations cope with transient advantages, we haven't yet come up with many humane ways of addressing the social adjustment problems this creates for people who were never trained to bear the burden of employment uncertainty themselves.

Is On-Demand Employment the Future of Work?

Mike Orchard, the founder of Skills Hive, wrote to me in response to a blog I wrote about the topic:

> I founded www.Skills-Hive.com in the UK last year to help more people and businesses understand the potential of the emerging employment models. While I agree that many people currently prefer to put their trust in a single employer to provide their security for them, an increasing number are keen to spread the risk and make their own decisions on pensions and healthcare. The benefits are not just with the employer, clearly all parties gain better control and increased agility, which is the key to success in our fast moving world . . . Personally, I have to agree with a great phrase coined by a young British entrepreneur, Brad Burton . . . "Having a job is just like having a business, except you only have one client—and how stupid is that?!"

I also heard from Brad Murphy, one of the executives at Gear Stream, a company that does high-end technology design and development work. He wrote:

> The nature of work is changing and many folks forget that the idea of a "job" is a relatively recent phenomenon that is an artifact of the master/slave model established during the industrial revolution. It is NOT the future of work (thank goodness). This current transition we're now in globally will likely take another 50 years to play out, but on the other side are some very exciting economic outcomes. Brave visionaries will pave the way in the interim. I am hopeful we will be one of those companies that builds a brighter future by creating new business models that are respectful and sustainable for all stakeholders—Individuals, Business Owners/ Shareholders, and the environment.

Despite these optimistic observations, however, it is clear that for many employees the concept of on-demand employment is highly problematic. The dark side of flexibility for employers is that it creates massive uncertainty for employees. In sectors such as retail, the *New York Times* reported massive changes:

> *"Over the past two decades, many major retailers went from a quotient of 70 to 80 percent full-time to at least 70 percent part-time across the industry," said Burt P. Flickinger III, managing director of the Strategic Resource Group, a retail consulting firm. The consequence for employees is unpredictable working hours, fewer hours than they would like to work, and a loss of benefits and predictability. This wreaks havoc upon their ability to maintain stable family lives and plan their own time.*[a]

a. S. Greenhouse, "A Part Time Life as Hours Shrink and Shift," *New York Times*, October 27, 2012.

Leverage External Resources Rather Than Building It All Yourself

Sometimes a company can get the critical resources it needs by joining forces with another organization to scale quickly. We have already seen examples of this in the case of Procter & Gamble's emphasis on "connect and develop," in which the company sources innovative ideas, often from smaller firms, and then uses its heft and scale to ramp them up and bring them to market quickly. Consultancy Accenture is another company that builds alliances with a number of technology leaders and innovators. Combined with its own industry expertise and skills at scaling operations, Accenture has been able to achieve formidable growth. The company has also had success building up external capabilities.

One of the more impressive success stories is a joint venture the firm began in 2000 with Microsoft, called Avanade. In an unusual move for a technology services firm, Avanade was created to focus on services that were based on Microsoft technology. The joint venture was announced in 2000. By the next year, it was operating in ten countries—a true global start-up—and had captured 120 of its large target customers and awarded 150 projects. By 2010, 11,000 people worked at Avanade. In ten years, the company had completed thousands of projects for hundreds of customers and had $1 billion in sales.

For the assets a company does decide to invest in, we are likely to see far greater emphasis on making sure that they can be disassembled and reconfigured as things change. This implies that rather than optimizing your asset configuration for a particular opportunity, you are more likely to prefer assets that can be flexibly redeployed. It's also important to watch out for getting stuck with assets that can create exit barriers later on. For instance, these might include factors that could force the company to reinvest capital assets, extensive interconnections and interdependencies with other businesses, substantial vertical integration, commitments to large numbers of stakeholders (such as unions or governments), codification of the business into written rules, or the potential for entrapment by customer demand later on (for instance, flood insurance or ATMs). As a general rule, in a transient-advantage context it is better to give up some optimization to create the advantage of flexibility.

The essence of this chapter has been to suggest that getting control of the resource allocation process is absolutely key to creating a deft organization that can cope with the effects of transient advantage. Having extracted resources from advantages that are fading away, it's time to put them to work creating new advantages. That is the task of the innovation process, to which we will turn in the next chapter.

5

Building an Innovation Proficiency

In far too many companies, the life of innovations resembles Thomas Hobbes's despairing characterization of the human condition: "nasty, brutish, and short." The fundamental problem is that in a world dominated by those pursuing exploitation, the innovation process is light amusement at best, a dangerous threat at worst. A broken innovation process guarantees that your organization will struggle to keep its edge as competitors catch up to whatever you were doing before. You should be thinking of how to avoid the cycle of success, decline, downsizing, near death, desperation, bet the company, and revival that characterizes so many corporate histories (such as Nokia, IBM, Procter & Gamble, and many others).

Innovation, like any other important organizational process such as quality management or safety, can be managed. Yet, for some reason when someone decides they want to become more innovative, they make it up as they go along, rather than learning what works and what doesn't. So before you let people blunder around reinventing the process every time someone gets the urge to innovate, it makes sense to understand it first. Fortunately, there are a lot of resources that you can use to become better informed about what innovation requires, which can be put into action right away, avoiding the unfortunately common mistakes.[1] The second thing to recognize is that on-again, off-again innovation, although very typical, is worse than doing nothing.[2] It sends the signal to good people that these are not the kind of projects they should bet their careers on, and it wastes resources. So, if you want to get it right, innovation needs to be continuous, ongoing, and systematic. Set aside a regular budget for it. Make it part of good people's career paths. Actively manage a portfolio in which innovations are balanced with support for the core business. And build it into the organizational processes that sustain anything else that is important in your company (see table 5-1).

TABLE 5-1

The new strategy playbook: innovation proficiency

From	To
Innovation is episodic	Innovation is an ongoing, systematic process
Governance and budgeting done the same way across the business	Governance and budgeting for innovation separate from business as usual
Resources devoted primarily to exploitation	A balanced portfolio of initiatives that support the core, build new platforms, and invest in options
People work on innovation in addition to their day jobs	Resources dedicated to innovation activities
Failure to test assumptions; relatively little learning	Assumptions continually tested; learning informs major business decisions
Failures avoided and undiscussable	Intelligent failures encouraged
Planning orientation	Experimental orientation
Begin with our offerings and innovate to extend them to new areas	Begin with customers and innovate to help them get their jobs done

What Innovation Proficiency Looks Like: Revisiting the Growth Outliers

In chapter 2, we had a look at the growth outliers—those unusual firms that have somehow managed to create proficiency at handling every aspect of the transient-advantage wave. What we saw in those firms is that they had built in ways of reconfiguring their businesses, by exiting exhausted opportunities and entering new ones, with the result that they combine stability and dynamism.

In researching these companies, it is clear that they have developed proficiency at managing each aspect of the innovation system, although they each do it a bit differently, of course. The core elements, however, are all there. This includes a governance system, and systems for ideation, for discovery and assumption testing, for market validation and incubation, and finally for commercialization and incorporation of the new businesses into their ongoing operations.

Overall Framework and Roles

In many cases, efforts to become innovative are doomed from the start because there isn't a clear overall framework within which innovation should occur. Roles are not clear, the governance and funding models are ill-specified, the specific activities of champions are left vague, and so on. In companies with an innovation proficiency, these matters are not left to chance. To be proficient, an organization needs a governance mechanism suitable for innovation (and usually separate from the planning and budgeting processes of the core business), a way of managing the resources devoted to innovation, an overall sense of how innovations fit into the larger portfolio, and a line of sight to initiatives in all different stages of development.

At Cognizant, one of the growth outliers, the overall framework is actually called the "managed innovation framework," which spells out the different roles that are essential for innovations to occur. The company combines both top-down and bottom-up approaches to innovation, but makes it clear who is supposed to do what. As it says on its website, vision and enablement are steered by senior leadership. This includes laying out the strategy of the firm, specifying what types of innovation are desirable, and supplying resources. The so-called middle level in the organization owns and drives initiatives. This involves figuring out how to get new activities to work with existing ones, doing the political work of building coalitions and alliances, and making sure that desirable initiatives are appropriately resourced. At the level of a specific initiative, an entrepreneurial team does the work of creating new business transactions and driving them into the marketplace.

Cognizant supports this framework with a heavy-duty dose of technology. Ideas are tracked and communicated using its proprietary Innovation Management System software, which connects to its Cognizant 2.0 corporate knowledge management system. Innovation, in other words, is not treated separately from other significant tasks within the firm; rather it is connected to other ongoing activities in a holistic way. Similarly, Indra Sistemas has a system it calls the Indra method for development, adaptation, and services (MIDAS in Spanish), which integrates new projects with the overall project management process within the firm.

One of the most formal and structured of the governance systems for innovation amongst the outliers is that of the ACS Group's environment business. It develops a strategic plan for what it calls R&D+i, meaning research, development, and innovation projects. It reviews plans annually or biannually, in a process that sets priorities and funding. Its formal management system is actually certified under the UNE 166002:2006 standard and audited by an independent third party. As ACS reports, as of December 31, 2011, there were twenty-eight research and development projects in progress, in which €5.62 million were invested.

Ideation

The goal of the ideation process is to identify a pipeline of promising ideas that a company might consider as vectors for their innovation effort. It encompasses the processes of analyzing trends, connecting innovations to the corporate strategy, scoping potential market opportunities, and eventually defining arenas in which a company may want to participate. Effective innovation begins with a clear definition of where it should be focused. Unfortunately, in many companies, particularly those who have bought into the "let a thousand flowers bloom" concept, it isn't clear what kinds of new ideas should be targeted.

Companies such as Google (and, historically, 3M) operationalize this theory by giving employees time at work to do whatever they want, without restriction or guidance. Everybody in the organization has the potential to be an innovator, we are told, and "no idea is a dumb idea." Well-intentioned efforts of this kind usually begin with enthusiastic cheerleading at the executive level. People are told to dedicate a portion of their time to pursuits that interest them and that are not part of their day jobs. Trainers are brought in to teach everybody to be innovators. There are "innovation boot camps." It works—ideas come pouring forth from every nook and cranny. Unfortunately, there *is* such a thing as a bad idea. Most won't lead to large enough opportunities to merit the investment. Many are half-baked and impractical. Often, as Tony Ulwick of Strategyn notes, they are not connected to customer outcomes. Others are a poor strategic fit. Others will anger supply chain partners or important vendors. And so it goes. The ideas go nowhere. The effort eventually withers on the vine, the people who were most excited about the initiative get discouraged or cynical, and the lessons learned evaporate.

This is a lot like the old joke about an infinite number of monkeys: put enough monkeys in a roomful of typewriters and eventually they will produce *War and Peace*. The difficulty is that nobody has enough money or time for an infinite supply of monkeys, and in fast-moving competitive markets an inefficient innovation process could be your undoing.

Companies have discovered far greater power in an approach—variously called the "jobs to be done" perspective,[3] "challenge-driven innovation,"[4] or "needs-driven innovation"[5]—in which customer needs are inputs to a "growth factory," as my colleague Scott Anthony argues.[6] The core idea is that the starting point for innovation should be figuring out what outcome customers are really seeking and working backward into how your organization might make that outcome happen. Note the difference: unlike the ideas-first approach, in which thinking, often internally driven, generates innovation projects, the jobs-to-be-done perspective starts with what customers want to accomplish, but can't get done. And of course, customers are notorious for being unable to articulate a need until they are shown how it can be met.

The growth outliers are specific about the kinds of ideas that fit their strategy. Infosys, for instance, is very focused on which types of clients it will serve and which it will not. The company focuses on high-growth industry segments and on the "reference" clients within them. It enjoys more than 97 percent repeat business, and has a philosophy that "our growth is a function of our client's growth," as Kris Gopalakrishnan explained to me. It refuses to pursue business (even though there are big volumes to be had) that doesn't involve value-added for its clients in some meaningful way, rather than simply benefit from labor cost arbitrage.

Infosys then aligns the incentive structure of its people around these characteristics. Sanjay Purohit, its head of strategy, terms this "micro-segmenting." He explains, "The goal is to improve the rate at which your business grows and how significant you are as a percentage of the whole company's revenue. By micro-segmenting . . . it drives behavior across businesses of the need to create value, and become relevant to more customers." Notice that identification of customer priorities comes first. A second "axis," as Purohit terms it, is in the portfolio of products and services. Each year, he notes, Infosys incubates and lays out new lines of offerings with the explicit understanding that it will take three years to get significant growth. For example, the company has recently announced three new initiatives—sustainability, customer mobility, and cloud—with the understanding that they will be growth drivers in the future.

At ACS Group's environmental business, the broad themes the company seeks to pursue are making maximum use of the energy that can be extracted from wastes, minimizing dumping, and reducing atmospheric emissions and odors. Krka seeks to use innovation to add value to its portfolio of off-patent drugs, increasing the value it offers to patients beyond the raw molecule rather than being a commodity producer of off-patent pharmaceuticals.

Note that the ideation process is never done once and finished—it needs to be an ongoing process of filling a pipeline of possibly good ideas. In our book *The Entrepreneurial Mindset*, we suggested the concept of an opportunity inventory, and that's still an idea worth considering.[7]

Discovery: Concept and Detailed Planning

With the seed of an idea in hand, the next process for proficient innovation is the process of discovery, in which concepts are fleshed out and detailed plans are developed. During the discovery process, specific customer needs are understood, arenas are sized and assessed for attractiveness, different business models are evaluated, and a rough framework for the business is created. In the detailed planning stage, assumptions are articulated and tested, a formal business plan and operational logistics may be developed, and key checkpoints are plotted out. The goal is to convert assumptions to knowledge as quickly and cheaply as possible. My previous coauthored book, *Discovery-Driven Growth*, offers a lot of detail on this process.[8]

If one examines the innovation process at Cognizant, one can see how the company has used technology to effectively support its discovery process. It has a system, called the idea management system, that allows the firm to track ideas and innovations, connect those who have knowledge that might be relevant to the innovation teams, test assumptions, and refine the ideas, all the while facilitating measurement and monitoring of what it calls "innovation scorecards."

At FactSet, the discovery process is embedded in the company's DNA. Its founders, Howard Wille and Charles Snyder, left their Wall Street jobs in 1978, as they later said, to "test their idea for a company that could deliver computer-based financial information." Thirty-one years later, the company has boasted uninterrupted revenue growth. A series of case studies on the company's website illustrates how it develops new offers by doing the discovery and detailed planning in close association with clients.

Incubation: Market Experimentation and Validation and Business Model Implementation

The incubation process of an innovation involves learning what the real business needs to be like. At this stage, pilots and prototypes are developed, market tests are conducted, and massive numbers of assumptions are tested. Initial customers and partners are engaged, and a dedicated team works exclusively on the project. The project is still vulnerable and fragile, but at this stage it begins to assume more substance as the prototypes become closer to a viable offer in the marketplace.

It is all too common for companies to rush through this phase, curtailing the valuable learning of what the ultimate product or service might look like. Another trap is to try to impose corporate demands for profits or growth on the fledgling business too quickly. Clayton Christensen said it best: "At this point in the development of an offer, one needs to be 'hungry for profits but patient for growth.'"[9] The offering is not yet ready for the full onslaught of commercial activity. Early adopters may put up with its inevitable deficiencies, but eventual mass market or mainstream customers will not. The best early markets are those customers who have a real, substantive need or problem that they will gratefully pay to have addressed. HDFC's foray into offering banking to rural villages offers an example.

HDFC Bank has a long tradition of carefully piloting new initiatives before making a major commitment to them. Its recent partnership with Vodafone to introduce banking access to financially excluded rural Indians is illustrative. The bank started by understanding the problem it wished to address, which is that in many parts of rural India there is simply no banking infrastructure. Further, other infrastructure, such as transportation and electricity, is not well developed either. As a local paper observes, "A farmer in Jhalsu village loses a whole day's earnings if he goes to a bank branch, a couple of km away, for a simple transaction like depositing or withdrawing cash."[10]

What HDFC and Vodafone piloted in that isolated, rural village was a system in which HDFC Bank uses select Vodafone retailers to represent the bank as subagents, enabling anyone to send money or withdraw cash through Vodafone's outlets. An HDFC Bank mobile bank account would allow the farmer to deposit cash that can then be withdrawn later or sent to another person, who in turn can go to a Vodafone outlet and collect the money. The service is much less expensive than prevailing alternatives, such as a money order processed via the post office. Having piloted the service in Jhalsu, leaders from HDFC Bank and Vodafone joined K. C. Chakrabarty, the deputy governor of the Reserve Bank of India, to announce the national rollout of the concept under the umbrella idea of supporting financial inclusion. HDFC Bank anticipates significant growth from rural ventures such as this one.

Acceleration: Commercialization, Launch, and Ramp-up

A final step in the innovation process is when an idea actually gets to market and is scaled up to a commercial reality. This is a delicate moment for an innovation project, because it marks a major transition point. At this point, the innovation and incubation emphasis needs to transition to mechanisms for getting to scale, fast. The business that has been protected from conventional disciplines (such as producing return on investment) now has to begin to be measured by conventional metrics, reporting structures and disciplines need to be put in place, managers with a different mind-set start to become more important, and the business needs to become part of the parent corporation. Often, the governance of the concept has to transition from the group doing piloting and concept validation to a business manager, whose measures and performance metrics are more conventional. The key issue is to manage this transition without losing the differentiation of the business itself.

Commercialization and scale-up are particular strengths of Cognizant. Pursuing a strategy in which it has explicitly told investors that it will sacrifice some margin to sustain strong growth, it doubles down on investments made to create a compelling result in specific arenas it seeks to penetrate. Its CEO, Francisco D'Souza, was reported in 2009 to have said that he regretted that he didn't invest in growth even more aggressively. As a reporter observed about the company's approach to scaling up fast, "It meant putting more people on the ground; getting them to spend more time with a specific set of must-have customers, disproportionate to the revenue they might account for at that specific point of time; taking on projects which might not give high margins initially, but might eventually become big; investing more resources on a specific project compared to what peers do and so on. All these meant that Cognizant was constantly grabbing more market share."[11]

How a Pure-Play Transient-Advantage Firm Manages Innovation

Introducing Sagentia

Cambridge-based Sagentia is a technical consultancy that to me exemplifies how companies can harness continual innovation to thrive, despite the coming and going of a particular competitive advantage. The lobby of Sagentia's offices in hard-to-find-unless-you're-local Harston Mill makes it quite clear that this is no run-of-the-mill suburban office complex. To your left is a glassed-in display area where what looks like the modern equivalents of medieval torture implements are displayed. Upon inspection, one learns that these are among the products Sagentia scientists and engineers have been instrumental in bringing into the world. All around you are colorful walls and soaring staircases, with windows onto flowering gardens. Although you have probably never heard of the company, its inventions are present in products that are today core to everyday life, in consumer as well as industrial products. One is led to a meeting room by a personal escort and politely asked to stay exactly where you are put, because what is going on around you is all top secret.

At Sagentia, innovation is clearly at the top of the agenda, through-out its operations. As one senior executive noted, "Inherently, com-panies like ours are super agile, because we are not in control of our own destiny . . . We can only live off something that our clients have decided to do." This makes Sagentia a model for where more and more businesses are headed—as competitive advantages shorten and competition comes from everywhere, increasingly firms are in the same position, that is, "not in control of [their] own destiny." Consistent, ongoing innovation and extraordinary closeness to customers is the only possible response.

The company has clearly identified sectors, or areas of interest in Sagentia-speak, and information gathering is confined to these areas, which fall under medical products, consumer products, and industrial products. As their joint managing director explained, "We use our sector organization to define our market agenda." The sector organization provides a set of fairly fluid containers for the talents and capabilities in the organization. The sector heads, in turn, are deep experts on the concerns of potential clients in their sectors.

Sagentia's leaders' dedication to identifying meaningful customer needs is palpable. As Dan Edwards, a joint managing director, explained to me, "We are a projects (not a product) organization. We earn money when we understand our customers' needs and impress them with our response. We are tested every day and put customer needs (not our assets) first in our thinking." Identification of a market need comes first. For example, the company has been following a major trend in what it calls "life science meets lifestyle," in which individuals are more and more going to be responsible for some or all of their health care services, often in a home-like setting. This trend will lead to entirely new categories of medical devices and treatment options, and Sagentia wants to be right there when the opportuni-ties arise.

The amount of information the company's executives sift through is staggering. Some 300 to 400 accounts of client meetings with salespeople and executives in the company are circulated each *month*. Senior executives, as part of their normal responsibilities, are expected to be very much on top of what is going on in their sectors. This includes reading trade journals, attending conferences, networking among key users, and "talking to people in a wide variety of scenarios." The managing directors, similarly, spend significant time networking, leveraging the different vantage points they bring relative to the other executives. The company employs librarians who prepare e-mailed reports on companies, technologies, and trends that Sagentia consultants might need to know.

Niall Mottram, who works in the consumer sector, observes that the company uses qualitative techniques as much as quantitative ones for finding meaningful customer jobs to be done. "Take something simple like a domestic coffee maker," he told me. "How people actually use that product can differ dramatically from how the designer envisaged it. People put in bottled water. They create their own flavorings. They double brew the coffee for extra strength." The insights from in-the-field observations are captured by someone who knows a lot about human factors partnering with people who are more technologically oriented.

In addition to trying to understand particular customer needs, the company is good at seeing patterns that may cut across its businesses. Information gathered through its extensive probes into the outside world is organized into a central repository, which is sifted through by a dedicated person in marketing. This role—of cross-silo information gathering—is missing in many organizations. What the marketer is looking for in particular are trends that cut across Sagentia's various operating areas. For example, a trend that the company is monitoring with "high-level pattern recognition" concerns personalization. Mottram offers personalization as a "macro trend" that Sagentia is expecting will influence the design of many of its future products. This applies even in services; as Mottram says, "People don't want the same level of care that Joe Bloggs had half an hour before." They want something individualized. Another macro trend is visualization, in which a surgeon might want to have both three-dimensional visualization within a procedure as well as a tactile feel in his or her fingertips, even when manipulating a robot or using a remote control.

Sagentia's choice of projects exemplifies an approach to competition that is radically different from conventional companies. First, they work on new-to-the-world problems of great complexity. As one senior executive said to me, " . . . we should be doing the stuff that is really hard to do, that is worth the money, which carries a premium of time or risk or technical complexity. Very few companies can do that. When we see lower level competition coming, that would be an early warning that it is not a good opportunity. It can be quite early in the life of that technology to the world, but it's coming to an end for us." Companies that escape the trap of established competitive advantage tend to have the capacity to create categories that are entirely new. Conventional concepts of competitive advantage have very little traction in such arenas.

Having decided a need is worth going after, Sagentia then mobilizes resources in a flexible, creative manner. According to Edwards, "All of our staff are operating in an internal free market— once a sector allocates a project, it has the pick of the staff from cross-functional groups (physics, electronics, mechanical engineering, chemistry, etc.). It's very unlike a product company where, say, 90 percent of resources are allocated to legacy brands and/or products."

The organizational structure changes as the projects the company works on change. This is vastly different from the way many companies are organized, and far friendlier to innovation. When I asked one of the sector heads for the most important advice he could give to other companies, he said, "You want to be mindful that you are not fulfilling your company's structure needs. You are fulfilling the needs of the market. In many companies, company structure becomes more important than world demand."

So far, we've explored the elements of innovation proficiency—managing the whole innovation process as a system, from governance through to scale-up and re-integration with the core business—and tried to understand how these processes are addressed in the growth outlier companies and Sagentia, a company that lives or dies by a constant flow of innovations. But by definition, the growth outliers are rare. Their success at getting innovations into the marketplace over time is, again by definition, unusual. So what about the rest of us—companies and organizations that don't necessarily have proficiency already or that have a sneaking feeling they could do better?

How Do You Build Innovation Proficiency if You Don't Have It?

Often, companies that want to become more innovative begin with a number of small-scale experiments with innovation and diversification. While there is no harm in experimenting this way, for these efforts to have a substantial impact on a large organization, the innovation effort would need to be given the same emphasis and attention as any other large-scale corporate undertaking. Here's the problem: most people in large organizations are fully preoccupied with driving the core business. They're already working long hours and grappling with crises on a day-to-day basis.

Moreover, what many companies don't realize is that crucial aspects of the innovation system require real expertise that needs to be built up over years. Trend analysis, market sizing, options analysis and valuation, designing prototypes, creating discovery-driven plans, running pilots, leveraging opportunities, and making the transition to a scalable business are all activities that take time, effort, and experience to get good at. In most companies, there is simply no career path that consistently helps people to develop these skills.[12] And in most companies, even if someone were to try to develop these skills, there are few rewards for doing so.

An obvious solution is to partner with organizations in which people spend their time doing nothing but living, breathing, and working on innovative ideas, in which there is spare capacity to implement the ideas you've come up with, and in which there is sound knowledge of what can go wrong and what to do when it does. Firms such as Innosight; IDEO; Accenture's growth group, Strategyn; and Cameron Associates (a consultancy that my coauthor Ian MacMillan and I are part of) are all organizations that I've observed do great jobs helping their clients tackle situations in which the innovation process breaks down. If your goal is to build innovation proficiency quickly while making a minimum number of mistakes, it can really help to bring some expertise to bear on the effort. Let me walk you through what an engagement with such a firm might look like.

Step 1: Assess the Current State of Things and Define the Growth Gap

The first thing you need to do is get a baseline and figure out what is actually going on. One way to do this is to analyze your portfolio of initiatives. A model for doing this is explained in detail in my previous coauthored book *Discovery-Driven Growth*—I'll briefly review it here.[13] The first thing is to think of the world in terms of two kinds of uncertainty. The first is uncertainty about markets—both internal and external. The second is uncertainty about the capabilities or technologies that you might deploy in various projects. The model suggests that you allocate projects to five different categories (see figure 5-1).

Core enhancements are projects and initiatives that help today's business better serve today's customers. In the language of the model, market uncertainty and technological uncertainty are relatively low. Core enhancements allow you to become faster, better, cheaper, more productive, or more accurate or are easier to use and more convenient. The purpose of the core business is to generate enough revenue so that you can pursue your

FIGURE 5-1

An opportunity portfolio

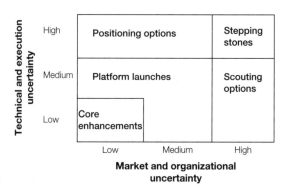

growth goals. If the core is not working well, that is job number one to fix.

Investments in new platforms, which generally have somewhat more uncertainty to them but are not bold leaps off into the wildly unknown, can be thought of as your next core business. These are generally projects that are in the scale-up stage of the innovation process. They represent future contributions to the core business.

The third category of investments is in options. Options are generally small investments you make today that buy you the right, but not the obligation, to make a more substantive investment in the future. Pilots, prototypes, early-stage experiments, living lab designs, and so on are all options. I like to think of options in three categories:

- **Positioning options** consist of initiatives in which you know there is a demand, but what is unknown is what combination of technologies and capabilities will be required to address that demand. Mobile devices such as smartphones in the United States are a bit like this—because there is no overall standard for wireless service, handset makers need to keep their options open by maintaining access to various types of standards.

- **Scouting options** are situations in which you have a capability or technology that you know how to use, and what you are trying to do is extend its reach into a new arena. That could be a new customer segment, a new geography, or a new application. Initiatives in this stage require a fair amount of prototyping and testing before you learn what will ultimately work. Apple, for example, built a mock-up of its retail store format and rigorously tested every aspect of the experience before rolling out its actual stores.

- **Stepping stones** are situations in which you think there will be a demand, and think the technology will eventually be

point, we went to the leadership group—the ones with the corporate checkbooks—to get the ideas funded. Thud. We had just made a profound mistake, which was not engaging the leadership from the beginning and not creating a strategic framework within which the ideas had to fit. The great new ideas were often not consistent with leadership's priorities. No way were they putting money into this weird new stuff when they had important near term priorities to tackle. The ideas went nowhere. You can imagine how demoralized and dispirited the teams were—indeed, we had made things worse by creating excitement without following through. Since then, I recommend that any growth effort begin by establishing the leadership framework within which innovation needs to operate.

In terms of reinforcing mechanisms, I like to further insist that if innovation really is important to the organization, then it will show up in its meeting agendas, on its website, and other places where it is visible to the organization that this is something that really matters.

Step 3: Set Up an Innovation Governance Process

The next logical step is to organize the way in which innovations will be governed. The most common approach to doing this is to set up an innovation board, which is often a group of senior business leaders. The purpose of this board is to hear project proposals, ask the right guiding questions, give projects the green light, and, if necessary, help to shut them down in the most constructive way if they aren't going to work out. The innovation board's other major task is to clear away bureaucratic and structural hurdles that will hamper the efforts of innovation teams. A single phone call from a senior person can sometimes resolve problems that would take weeks to work out in a peer-to-peer context. At IBM, innovation governance was a mainstream responsibility with a senior person reporting to the CEO in charge.

As part of the innovation governance process, a definition of the opportunity spaces the organization is prepared to explore is developed. This provides clarity on what kinds of ideas are desirable (and which are not) and helps guide the innovation effort.

Step 4: Start Building a System and Introducing It to the Organization

Just as with any other organizational process—say, six sigma—there are practices that work well when it comes to innovation and those that don't. It is helpful to have a critical mass of people in the organization understand what some of those practices look like, even if they are not going to be responsible for doing the actual innovating. Training is usually the preferred vehicle to do this, and it can take many forms. I've done in-house classes, seminars, webinars, virtual training, you name it. The key thing is that you want people to begin to have a common language for talking about innovation and the recognition that what works for business-as-usual doesn't work for innovation.

At Pearson, for example, the head of their clinical assessments business, Aurelio Prifitera, was concerned about renewing the business, even though it was, and is, very successful. In partnership with Krys Moskal, the vice president for people development, Prifitera initiated an effort to create a more systematic approach to innovation. We started with a day-long retreat with his leadership team to review basic innovation concepts. That meeting led to several initiatives: a portfolio analysis; the launch of an innovation board; allocation of resources to several new projects; and the funding of training and coaching to help people build up the skills needed for innovation. In the first year after that meeting, I led a series of fourteen teleseminars, running roughly two weeks apart, which could be attended by a broad mass of decision makers in the business (as Krys says brightly, "anybody has access to a phone, right?"). Some regular training such as that is crucial for developing skills and helping people create a common language.

Step 5: Start Off with Something Tangible and Real

At this point, it makes a lot of sense to pick one or more innovation ideas and begin to use the tools to develop those ideas. Often, this will involve a project that is already under way but struggling to get traction. The important thing is that the consultants or whoever you are using to support your effort have the chance to demonstrate proof of concept with something that is actually in the works. The practices of customer demand identification, market sizing, prototyping, business model design, discovery-driven planning, and all the other concepts that are specific to innovation come into play here.

What my colleagues Ron Pierantozzi and Alex van Putten of Cameron Associates learned—painfully—was that the way they thought they would be able to engage with an organization, after creating leadership buy-in, often didn't work. They thought that once the leadership team had given the innovation effort approval and allocated resources to it, the next logical step would be to have a big meeting with all the project people to introduce them to the core ideas. Here's the problem: by the time that meeting gets set up, months have often gone by. Just because people are now authorized to engage in innovation doesn't mean their calendars instantly clear and their other commitments disappear. Instead, what Ron and Alex learned was that they did better working in bottom-up mode, selecting a few teams to support on an ongoing basis, and then helping them through the discovery and incubation phases of the projects, which is often where current staff lack the time and expertise to do this work.

Step 6: Create the Supporting Structures for Innovation

Ideally, with early proof of concept that these techniques for innovation are useful, now is the time to start putting in place supporting structures. Dedicated teams to handle ideation, discovery, and incubation; IT systems (such as Cognizant's innovation management system) that help link people together; budget structures that operate with a real options sensibility, and so on, are all part of creating a complete system. My colleagues at Innosight call this building a "growth factory."[14] At this stage, the venture is usually transferred to the structures that will scale the business and ensure reliability.

The steps themselves are pretty straightforward. What you need to be prepared for, of course, is that the established, exploitation-oriented organization will tend to resist them at just about every turn. My recommendation is that you plan on a two- to three-year effort to get your innovation system in place. Once you do, however, the benefits are tremendous.

Building Innovation Proficiency Systematically at Brambles

To illustrate how the steps just discussed relate to a real organization, let's have a look at a process that Ron Pierantozzi and Alex van Putten used to support the efforts of Robert Spencer, the chief innovation officer at Australia's Brambles, over the past two years. Brambles runs a pretty unglamorous business, namely the circulation of pallets used to stock and move goods all over the world. Brambles was founded in 1875 by Walter Bramble, who was brought to Australia by his English parents when he was less than a year old. As an adult, he became a "cut up and deliver" butcher, meaning he would bring his products to customers. His company, subsequently called Bramble and Sons, increasingly concentrated on logistics, incorporating as a transport business in 1925 with the motto "Keep moving."

The modern firm had its start in a historical accident. The Allied Materials Handling Standing Committee was created by the Australian government to provide efficient handling of defense supplies during World War II. When the Americans left Australia at the end of the war, they left behind mountains of materials handling equipment, among them pallets and containers. Managing these assets fell to an organization called the Commonwealth Handling Equipment Pool (CHEP), which was run for some time by the government. Eventually, the government decided to privatize the industry, and CHEP was sold to Brambles in 1958. The modern Brambles has a pool of more than 400 million pallets and other types of containers that it manages for customers in more than 50 countries. In the 2012 financial year, it generated revenues of $5.6 billion. (Yes, billion—on the basis of moving pallets and other storage containers all around the world.)

Our story starts in 2009, when Tom Gorman became the CEO, having joined Brambles in 2008 to run the CHEP operations in Europe, the Middle East, and Africa the prior year after a long career at Ford Motor Company. At the time, he told a reporter, "We are going to grow through geographic expansion, new platforms and new service offerings but now you need to put a real strategy around that. That's what's ahead of us."[15] He was determined not only to pursue innovation but also to make it a systematic, institutional capability as part of his legacy at Brambles. Not that the company wasn't innovative already. As Rob Spencer, the company's director of innovation, explained to me, "If you drop a powerful person in the company who was passionate about an idea, that person could make it happen." What Gorman, who hired Spencer to drive the innovation effort, wanted to do instead was make innovation a systematic capability.

Gorman reached out to one of the world's leading experts on growth, who had by then moved to Australia, consultant and author Mehrdad Baghai.[16] Baghai suggested that Spencer work with Ron and Alex to create this systematic capability for innovation, which needed to be managed differently from the core business. They worked their way through the process I outlined in the previous section.

Step 1: Assess the Current State of Things and Define the Growth Gap

As Ron described the task at Brambles, "We start with trying to understand what they are trying to do. Companies will often say they want to be innovative, but you have to know what you are trying to accomplish." Once you have a sense of the growth goals (which were quite ambitious at Brambles), then you think through how much you can expect to get from external sources, such as M&A or venture investments, and how much needs to come from organic growth.

Step 2: Get Senior Management Alignment and Resource Commitment

With Gorman as an advocate, reasonably substantial funds were set aside to support the innovation process. These were corporate funds, not funds from individual businesses, to reduce the reluctance of business unit heads to be supportive. Another issue was to clarify what areas would be acceptable for innovation proposals. As Gorman had indicated at the outset, the scope for growth at Brambles would be focused on taking their intellectual property in pallet pooling and expanding that into new segments and geographies.

Step 3: Set Up an Innovation Governance Process

With an idea of how much growth they sought to get out of their innovation proposals, Gorman and Spencer set up an innovation board, which is an entity separate from business-as-usual governance structures.

There was some learning to be done, however. One problem the consultants ran into early on was that the CEO called the central fund an "innovation fund" and said the company was looking for more initiatives that had high uncertainty but that could also potentially have a big impact. As he observed later, "That language was just too restrictive," and the company had people coming up with things that didn't fit the criteria for being sufficiently innovative. He reflected later that "that caused some disillusionment." The company actually had trouble getting enough good ideas into the pipeline at the outset.

So the company shifted from simply saying there was a fund to being more explicit about what the company was looking to do. It articulated three broad areas that would define what was in scope to be funded by the innovation fund. The first would include projects that were potential revenue generators. Then there were value generators, which were defined as projects that increase margins, help to maintain premiums, reduce costs, or just create greater marketplace differentiation. A final category was insight generators, the front-end piece that helps the company understand new and emerging customer needs. Then, the firm established targets for what would come out of the innovation fund. As Spencer says, "We expect to review at least X of each of these, fund Y, and graduate Z each year to grow." To end the circular arguments about what was innovative and what was not, the company used five questions—if a project can answer "yes" on two of them, it is considered innovative enough to be a candidate for funding. The five questions are as follows:

1. Does the proposal represent a new operating model or business model?

2. Is it something that would open us up to new or different customers?

3. Does the idea expose us to potentially new competition or different competition?

4. Would it require new skill sets—do we need to recruit or train people to do it?

5. Would it require new technologies or types of resources or facilities or whatever that we don't know how to manage?

Today, there are similar boards to tackle more localized initiatives within the businesses, allowing for greater inclusiveness in the process and for more ideas to receive funding.

Step 4: Start Building a System and Introducing It to the Organization

With their experience as practicing executives (in the case of Ron, as the director of innovation at Air Products and Chemicals, Inc., and in Alex's case, as a financial whiz in three of his own companies and at Chrysler Capital Realty), Ron and Alex had had the job of creating innovation systems themselves. Since then, they have worked with a number of other organizations to do the same. The components they brought to Brambles included discovery-driven planning to build business cases and learning plans; opportunity-engineering to manage risk and account for option value; consumption chain analysis and attribute mapping to hone in on customer needs and opportunities; business model analysis to identify new business model opportunities; and many others.[17] The advantage of bringing in people experienced in building these innovation systems is similar to bringing in experts for anything else new to the organization—it's faster and less risky than trying to invent it all from scratch. (I'm writing about Ron and Alex because I'm familiar with their process, but there are other excellent consultancies for whom the same observations would apply.)

Among the benefits of working with people who have an external perspective are that they can help explain the financial side of innovation to people in the finance area; finance people have to be on board, philosophically. As a former finance executive, Alex can convincingly show how you can impose intelligent fiscal discipline on projects, even under high uncertainty, by employing options rationale and managing risks explicitly.

Another benefit of bringing in external expertise in building an innovation system is that you can acquire diverse points of view. At Brambles, Spencer was very keen to make sure that people's ideas were challenged and that issues were examined from different perspectives.

Step 5: Start Off with Something Tangible and Real

Initially, Ron and Alex were brought to Brambles to give training sessions on the innovation system tools. Rather than providing empty classroom exercises, however, Rob and his team decided to start applying innovation tools to an actual initiative. At that time, one of their businesses had spent a fair amount of money on what it called "track and trace" technologies, but the project didn't seem to be going anywhere. So it held a workshop, which Alex led, using the discovery-driven planning framework to work through the underlying logic of the program. As the teams worked through it, they came to the realization that what they had on their hands was a type of project that Alex, Ron, and I call the "living dead." These are projects that haven't quite failed, but haven't succeeded, and which will simply absorb time and effort as they lumber on, with no real hope for a change in their trajectory. As Spencer said somewhat ruefully, "It would have been valuable if we'd had discovery-driven planning at the beginning of the process, before we'd spent the money." It ended up being rational to wind it up and redirect the resources toward other endeavors.

Step 6: Create the Supporting Structures for Innovation

The first year that Ron and Alex were involved, as I mentioned, was mainly devoted to training. They would do training for intact project teams in a variety of places, bringing in three to five teams at a time for two- to three-day workshops. In the workshops, they would walk through learn-to-apply consumption chain analysis, business model development, discovery-driven planning, opportunity-engineering, the use of sensitivity analysis, and so on. Despite everybody's best intentions, however, the process wasn't getting the traction that Rob Spencer would have liked to have seen. As Ron says now, "We'd go in and work with the project teams, but never heard a lot after the fact." Actually, in my experience this isn't unusual. It typically takes a while before a critical mass of people in the organization develops a common language and point of view about innovation.

In the second year, Brambles decided to change the model from a "training" emphasis to more of a coaching role. So Ron and Alex began to coach various project teams through key checkpoints, testing of assumptions and developing learning plans. Ron and

Alex work with the innovation teams roughly on a quarterly basis, coaching them in how to test assumptions and how to think in a disciplined way about the projects. Ron told me the other day that "we just came back from a session in which we went through six projects—we ended up killing one, simply by doing the analysis and asking 'why are you doing this?'" Among the things Ron and Alex are trying to embed in the organization is the idea of pursuing multiple options, thinking in terms of different scenarios, and differentiating behavior when one is working on innovation as opposed to business as usual. Instead of just doing training, the goal now is to create forcing mechanisms that keep the teams applying the skills, which are now being transferred to internal people to build the skill set in-house.

As I mentioned, Brambles funds the early-stage ventures from a central corporate pot, which makes the investment for the businesses less risky and makes them less reluctant to get involved. Once the new businesses start to generate revenues and profits, they pay back to the core fund. If the businesses are discontinued before they get to that stage, the businesses owe corporate nothing. Rob Spencer notes that this has an important psychological effect. Instead of people feeling that they might have career trouble if they are involved with a venture that is discontinued, they instead see that it can be used for learning and that there is little stigma attached. Further, there is very little downside risk for the associated business.

Today, the corporate innovation board meets monthly. There are now innovation boards within the operating business units, and Rob Spencer and his team have engaged in the same kind of consulting with them. Brambles now has eight dedicated people around the world working on innovation practices, in Europe, the Americas, and the Asia-Pacific area.

Being Smart about Building Innovation Proficiency

It's worth noting a few things Brambles has done really well in developing its innovation capability. It hired and empowered a senior leader whose sole role is that of driving innovation, Rob Spencer. In all too many companies, innovation is either not a priority at all or, as Brambles previously found, is dependent on powerful people to aggressively champion an idea. Further, it set up a dedicated fund and governance mechanism to reduce the risk and potential for infighting among the business units. This also eliminates the chronic problem of new businesses being managed like more certain ones. Brambles also set up a measurement system to see how it is doing on implementation. As Ron says, "They track everything." The company has what it calls an "innovation dashboard," which tracks the following:

- Ideas submitted per month

- Sessions (workshops) held and on which topics

- Employees trained

- Ideas by category

- Status of the innovation fund in terms of total revenue opportunity

- Revenue opportunity by category

- Funds spent and returned to the innovation fund

- Opportunities received, opportunities funded, and opportunities launched

The value of a dashboard such as this is tremendous, both in keeping the innovation process tangible and fresh in people's minds and in showing progress over time and letting people know symbolically that senior leaders are paying attention.

Brambles has also tackled the issue of incentives to engage in innovation. As I mentioned, the first thing it did was to remove disincentives by tackling the resource question and issues of fear of failure. To provide positive incentives, one of the mechanisms is that the most senior people in the company—the CEO, CFO, and business heads—all sit on the innovation board. The teams with ideas get to present to these very senior people, people who they might not have an opportunity to get to know in the course of their normal day jobs. So if their ideas work, there is huge visibility right to the top of the company.

Examples of innovations that Brambles is exploring include targeting ways to tackle the "last mile" problem in groceries and fast-moving consumer goods companies. A tremendous amount of labor cost in the supply chain is eaten up by human beings taking materials from storage areas and stocking shelves. Brambles is trying to find solutions that can limit the amount of handling that materials require. An example that is already in the market (particularly in Europe) is to sell fruit and vegetables in plastic crates. Those products would have been placed right into the crate when they were picked, then shipped in the crates and simply placed on the shelves. As Rob Spencer says, "That's the kind of thing they're looking for in other areas." The company is also considering putting wheels on some pallets. The trouble is, as Rob notes, that retailers love the idea of wheels, and everybody else in the supply chain—logistics companies, manufacturers, producers—all hate them! So Brambles is considering whether it can come up with innovations that would give it the best of both worlds.

Although the journey at Brambles is ongoing (and has to date taken about two years), there are tremendous signs of progress.

The pace of ideation has picked up, and the ideas themselves are less incremental. Rob Spencer has created an increasingly skillful internal group that can work with project teams to use the appropriate practices for highly uncertain ventures. It has also taken on training duties itself. As Ron says, "Rob and his team help people craft and develop the ideas." Brambles's annual report notes with pride that the company is well on its way to creating a culture of innovation, and innovation is featured as a key strategic thrust in the company's 2011 annual report. Tom Gorman, in a recent TV interview, pointed with evident pride to Brambles's "growth in every business."[18] If you can do it in pallets, you can do it with anything.

Innovation Is Central to Strategy

Innovation is not optional in a world of fleeting advantages. Innovation is not a sideline. Innovation is not a senior executive hobby or a passing fad. Innovation is a competency that needs to be professionally built and managed. Where in years past we often thought of strategy only with respect to existing advantages, in a transient-advantage economy innovation can't be separated from effective strategy. Fortunately, we have a pretty good idea of the practices and procedures that allow you to do this successfully.

In this chapter, I've talked a bit about the importance of leadership to establishing the right processes for innovation. Effective leadership in a transient-advantage economy will also establish a different mind-set and approach than is appropriate to slower-moving spaces. In the next chapter, we'll examine the different mind-set leaders need to adopt if they are to be successful in a transient-advantage context.

6

The Leadership and Mind-Set of Companies Facing Transient Advantages

Leadership in a transient-advantage world calls for a shift in emphasis from the core businesses dominating the agenda to options being equally important. It also places a premium on the ability to generate continuous renewal and innovation. In a world of transient advantages, the ability to pick up on early warnings and to get the organization to pay attention is critically important (table 6-1).

The growth outliers proved adept at doing this, both in their recognition of where strategic opportunities would lie and how they would sequence their moves into these new spaces. Javier Monzon, the CEO of Indra Sistemas of Spain, laid out its plans explicitly. The company, created in 1993 from a consolidation of preexisting firms,

TABLE 6-1

The new strategy playbook: mind-set

From	To
Assumption that existing advantages will persist	Assumption that existing advantages will come under pressure
Conversations that reinforce existing perspectives	Conversations that candidly question the status quo
Relatively few and homogenous people involved in strategy process	Broader constituencies involved in strategy process, with diverse inputs
Precise but slow	Fast and roughly right
Prediction oriented	Discovery driven
NPV oriented	Options oriented
Seeking confirmation	Seeking disconfirmation
Internally focused on optimization	Aggressively focused on the external world
Talent directed to solving problems	Talent directed to identifying and seizing opportunities
Extending a trajectory	Promoting continual shifts
Accepting a failing trajectory	Picking oneself up fast

decided that step one in its strategy would be to create advantages in Spain, and then build outward from the Spanish market into more international markets. Its aspirations were always to be global, but the arenas with which it began were local. Then, it selected a few new markets in which to globalize, eventually by 2005 realizing its slogan "We want to be a company that can compete anywhere in the world."[1]

Will Existing Advantages Remain? A Moment of Truth at Kodak

Scientists are trained to do two things that managers are often not. The first is to interpret patterns in the evolution of the state of things. The second is to respect the truth, regardless of how inconvenient or controversial its implications are. Unfortunately, often the truths they tell fall upon deaf ears.

In 1979, a German-born research chemist, Wolfgang H. H. Gunther, was making an exciting career move from Xerox to Kodak. During the courtship phase of the discussions, Gunther was invited to give a presentation at Kodak. He gave a talk using overhead projector slides that were generated on the Xerox Alto (an early version of a personal computer, courtesy of Xerox PARC). Among the people he subsequently spoke with was an executive named Tom Whiteley, the head of Kodak's Emulsion Research Division. Whiteley asked how Gunther visualized the future of technology. As Gunther said to me, "And then I casually said: 'Of course, with video cassette recording cameras, 8-mm movies have already had it.' At which point I thought I had blown the interview because he, sort of, freaked out and berated me for not understanding how well-entrenched the Kodak technology was." Recall that this was 1979—the very year that the Hunt brothers tried to corner the silver market, with the result that Minoru Ohnishi of Fuji Photo began to think about a future without film. Gunther was already thinking of a future without film. The Kodak executives couldn't conceive of such a thing. Fuji, as we saw in chapter 1, was already determined to move to the next wave. Kodak's leaders couldn't bear the prospect, determined to continue to exploit the company's longstanding advantages in film.

At any rate, Kodak did make Gunther the offer and he went off to the Kodak labs, eventually received a prestigious research award (the CEK Mees Award for Scientific Excellence in 1982/1983), was listed as an inventor on over a hundred patents (assigned to Xerox, Kodak, Sterling, Nycomed, and Medical College of Wisconsin), and eventually retired after being caught up in multiple reorganizations following Kodak's disastrous foray into the pharmaceutical business. Whiteley, in a later-life avocation that can only be described as ironic, became a highly respected amateur paleontologist.[2] He spent his postretirement years studying creatures that died out because of their failure to adapt.

Absolute candor and a willingness to accept the idea that a once-successful model needs to change are critical to leadership in a transient-advantage-oriented firm. Denying problems wastes critical time. In 1984, five years after Gunther joined Kodak, a *Forbes* article with the title "Has the World Passed Kodak By?" summed up many of the issues the company faced at that time.[3] Instead of taking the article as a possible wake-up call, Kodak's management instead put together a seven-page, single-spaced series of rebuttals to the claims made in the article.[4] Calling the article a "cover-story hatchet job," the documents provided detailed counterarguments (under the word "Rebuttal," underlined and centered, just in case anyone missed the point). The concerns raised by the journalists concerned poor management, deteriorating financial performance, poor execution of new product introductions, low morale, being forced to source products externally, and miscellaneous other problems. The rebuttals took the unconvincing form of outright denials in the form of "Kodak does not have poor management" and "Current management has overcome any historical complacency regarding the company's ability to meet its growth and profitability objectives." The piece also expressed a traditional excuse for management whose companies are not doing well—blaming forces beyond their control.[5]

So here we are, as of this writing a good twenty-nine years after the "hatchet job," and Kodak has declared bankruptcy. The once-humming factories are literally being blown up, and the company's brand, which Interbrand had valued at $14.8 billion in 2001, fell off its list of the top one hundred brands in 2008, with a value of only $3.3 billion.[6] It really bothered me that the future was so visible in 1980 at Kodak, and yet the will to do anything about it did not seem to be there. I asked Gunther recently why, when he saw the shifts coming so clearly, he did not battle harder to convince the company to take more forceful action. He looked at me with some surprise. "He asked me my opinion," he said, "and I gave it to him. What he did beyond that point was up to him." Which is entirely characteristic of scientists like Gunther. They may see the future clearly, but are often not interested in or empowered to lead the charge for change. Why do I know this story so well? He happens to be my father.

Strategy making is often carried out by a small group of people without a great deal of input from the rest of the organization. That is risky. There is a profound lesson here for those entrusted with steering their organizations through uncertain patches. Often, the people who see changes coming are not those in charge of making major organizational decisions. They are technologists, scientists, and pattern recognizers. Often, also, the people who *are* in positions to make difficult choices face the prospect of personal and career catastrophe if the predictions turn out to be true.

Seeking Out the Tough-to-Hear Information

As Alan Mulally, currently the CEO of Ford, observed, "You can't manage a secret." Strategy in a transient-advantage context dramatically increases the importance and value of obtaining difficult, disconfirming information at both the organizational and personal level. Environments that can move from advantage to advantage will be rich in feedback flows, both down and up the chain of command. Allowing senior executives to become isolated from the reality of what is going on at the company's competitive arenas or allowing them to become protected from feedback about their own behavior will increasingly be recipes for disaster.

Alex Gourlay, Chief Executive of the Health and Beauty division of Alliance Boots, emphasized this point at a recent management conference. "How do we make sure that bad news travels faster?" he challenged his leadership team to ponder.

It is often surprisingly difficult for senior people to get unfiltered information. For instance, I once had in class a senior executive from a telecom provider that was known for its spotty coverage, particularly in the New York area. I asked him about why their senior leaders didn't appear to be more upset by this—weren't they also infuriated by dropped calls and missed connections? Oh, "No worries," I was told. "We know their travel schedules, their routes, and where they are likely to be when they visit. We always make sure the signals along those passageways are good and strong!" Ironically, in their effort to improve their bosses' connectivity, the (we hope) well-intentioned staff were depriving them of the very information they would need to correct massive customer outrage. I see it all the time: senior people are kept in an alternative reality, in which the issues and problems that affect their customers are buffered for them.

Diversity is also going to become critical. In a situation replete with complexity and unpredictability, one never knows where the next important idea will emerge. If the senior team is very homogeneous, it limits the amount of mental territory that they can cover, when contrasted with a team that brings more diverse perspectives in terms of age, gender, socioeconomic status, or other attributes. Diversity in unpredictable contexts is not a "nice to have"—it will increasingly become competitively essential.

It will also be vital to combine different skills in the senior team and the rest of the organization. Not everybody is going to have a skill set that can effectively operate in each phase of the wave. Some people are more comfortable with the ambiguity and learning-rich environments of the innovation and launch stages. Some enjoy bringing order and stability to a large business, as we might find in the ramp-up phase. Some—many traditional leaders—will be brilliant at exploitation. And some might even be good at disengagement and reconfiguration. Being more explicit about the different skills and roles people bring to the tasks will be crucial. As Kris Gopalakrishnan of Infosys noted, each of the company's founders took a different role in the early company, with some leaders focusing on marketing, others on building technology platforms, others on operations, and so on.

In any case, getting beyond denial that there is a problem has to be part of a mind-set to cope with transient advantage.

Reinvigorating the Core Business at Berlitz

I have had personal encounters with Berlitz on a couple of different dimensions. It all started with a decision on the part of my daughter, Anne, and me to take German lessons—together. I wanted to improve what our teacher resignedly calls my "kitchen German," and Anne was interested in adding another European language to her repertoire. We signed up for intensive German lessons—as often as three times a week for three hours each—at the Berlitz on-site studio in Princeton, New Jersey.

Berlitz sure didn't make it easy. When I first called to set up the series, I was told that I would have to make an appointment and come in to the office in person, just to schedule the course. Well, given my travel schedule, that pushed things back by three weeks! When we finally did get in, we were presented with a fixed menu of options, and very expensive options at that. Although we loved Charlie Townsend, our teacher, we seemed to be struggling with Berlitz policy all along the way. Whether it was asking Charlie to teach us grammar ("I'll do it," he said, "but don't tell *them* that, because it isn't the Berlitz method!") or trying to figure out a schedule that worked for us, or figuring out whether I could find a way to continue the lessons once Anne went back to school, the company was one big, inflexible, grumpy old organization.

Our experiences were typical—Berlitz was very hard to do business with. Its performance showed; when contrasted with hip, upbeat competitors such as Rosetta Stone, with its ubiquitous ads about glamorous Italian supermodels being wooed by American farm boys, Berlitz looked downright dowdy. Rosetta Stone was gearing up for an IPO; Berlitz was treading water. In transient-advantage terms, Berlitz was well on its way to a long, slow, deadly period of erosion of its competitive advantages.

I got to thinking about Berlitz from a strategy point of view when I met Marcos Justus, at the time Berlitz's head of operations in Brazil. Justus is tall, razor thin, and intense. He speaks English ever-so-slightly accented with Portuguese (his native language, one of several that he speaks fluently), and when he gets excited, his thoughts seem to race ahead of his ability to get the words out. He's constantly looking for new ideas, and when he finds one he likes, he grabs on to it with ferocious intensity and will not let go. The quest for new ideas brought him to my Columbia Business School short course, "Leading Strategic Growth and Change." He still gives the course and the people he met in it credit for helping him reinvigorate the business in Brazil. Rather than positioning Berlitz as a simple language training company, he changed the branding and positioning to that of a luxury brand. Brazil, like many emerging economies, he reasoned, had a few really wealthy people at the top of the economic pyramid. Why not target the company to serve them? Advertisements changed from common or garden-variety ads for language proficiency to ads showing elegantly dressed women carrying their Berlitz materials out of their Audis to go to class—that sort of thing. It worked.

Based on his success in Brazil, Justus was asked to help reinvigorate the company's US operations. I went and chatted with him at Berlitz's offices near Princeton, New Jersey. The denial stage was long gone by this time, and everyone knew the company was having problems. The first challenge was figuring out what to fix. One of his insights about the United States was that language skill training in America is a "nice to do," not a "need to do." As he explained, in most of the world, if you can't speak English, it is a career setback, so selling language training is relatively easy. In the United States, however, you have to create a need. So where to start? Berlitz keeps track of everyone who calls to inquire about a course. What Justus found was that for every ten inquiries the company received, only three people actually signed up. So the first thing he started to do was survey those who did not convert. What the survey-takers basically were told was that the company was too expensive, too inflexible, and not innovative. As he said, "It was kind of depressing, but we had a huge opportunity—there was lots to do."

He and his team set about doggedly tackling the problems of expense, flexibility, and innovation by introducing new formats, new products, new delivery models, and new pricing structures. The goal was to reinvigorate the basic offering as a place to start. He eliminated the rigid Berlitz schedule requirements (most of which grew up over time to suit the teachers, not the students) in new products such as "Berlitz Connect." Lessons can be face to face or virtual. They can be recorded. A cultural component has been added, as well as quizzes and the chance to replay lessons that may not have sunk in. The fees can be paid by subscription (as opposed to the traditional Berlitz up-front payment plan). The company also introduced the "Berlitz Virtual Classroom," which makes group pricing and interaction costs possible even for people who are widely dispersed. Justus told me about how this led to a thriving business in Arabic. As it happens, some 1,500 inquiries per year in the

United States were for Arabic language lessons, but they were too spread out for the traditional Berlitz group-class approach. By combining the students virtually, people who never could have become customers were now signing up.

Rather than sticking with the original, proven model, Justus has invigorated the business in the near term. For the longer run, Berlitz's new CEO seeks to position the company as a cultural training organization and a global education company that can partner with your company to have a global-ready team. Think of it like a pyramid with language at the base. Then comes cultural understanding. Following that is what the company calls diversity and inclusion, and then global leadership skills.

The company has also taken a fresh approach to its brand, using humor to promote the idea of language proficiency. In one viral video with millions of YouTube hits, a member of the German Coast Guard is seen responding to a desperate plea on the radio:

"May Day, May Day, we are sinking!"

"Hallo—Zis is ze German Coast Guard."

"We're sinking, we're sinking!"

"What . . . what are you sinking about?"

The scene cuts immediately to the phrase "Improve Your English," set against a backdrop of stirring music and the tag line "Berlitz, Language for Life."

You Can't Manage a Secret: Seek Disconfirmation Rather Than Confirmation

Psychologists tell us that we all have a pervasive bias in our thought processes, namely, to seek out information that confirms what we believe to be true and to reject information that calls what we think is so into question. It's called the confirmation bias. The organizational analogue is to seek confirmatory evidence that all is well. Part of the new playbook for strategy is to do what Justus did at Berlitz and actually seek out disconfirming evidence. The idea is to create an environment in which people can share evidence that things may be changing and thereby spark action. This can be easier when it is obvious that the organization is in trouble—it's much harder when things seem to be going well, at least on the surface.

The data is often there, if anyone cares to look. The question then becomes who in the organization has the credibility and clout to get those in power to pay attention. There are a number of ways this can happen. The first is to drive it from the top, with strong CEO decision making. If the implications of a change in strategy are personally challenging or risky for other senior leaders, this is often the only way to do it. A friend of mine, a consultant, tells a story about one of the most dreadful projects he ever worked on—as it happens, for a telecom company facing the advent of the digital age. As he described it, the company was asking the consultancy team to help think through how it could remain relevant. The team recommended something similar to the strategy that Verizon has subsequently pursued, a FIOS-type play. The proposal had to be presented to the top thirty people in the company. As he put it, "The new organization we designed needed only four senior-type people. So you're going to get twenty-six people to vote to eliminate their own jobs? It was doomed from the start." Unlike Verizon's Seidenberg, the CEO at that firm was a "consensus guy"—what was missing was a CEO who would drive the new strategy. That company, incidentally, has since disappeared, swallowed up in the wave of subsequent telecom mergers, and those senior folks who opposed the radical changes the consultants recommended lost their jobs anyway.

A second approach is to empower a group—insiders, outsiders, or some combination—whose primary purpose is to gather the evidence, sift it, and feed the resulting insights back to the decision makers in the firm. My friend from a medical device company explained that his firm has just recently set up a disruptive analysis group to consider the question of how the company's business model could be disrupted. It has an organization and a budget that is separate from the rest of the mainstream business. So that's an independent group, with dedicated funding.

You can also use experts to find those early warnings. Doug Smith is a dear colleague and an expert on how companies can go awfully wrong after being stunningly successful (his excellent book about Xerox, *Fumbling the Future*, is a classic).[7] I asked him what he would do to break through to those who have decision-making rights in a company facing eroding advantage. He thoughtfully suggested that companies have specific conversations with experts about how sustainable the sources of advantage are. As he said, "Perhaps I would start a new management process in our company—the 'sustainable advantage review' process. I would call it out and separate it from the others. It needs a special light." He then suggested sponsoring a conference in which experts were invited in and paid to explain exactly how the company's existing advantages could be undermined.

Another way to unlock vital information is to work with internal networks. Tom Roy, an American, at one point held a remarkable position as the senior executive human resource director for French company Michelin. His approach to getting the word out can only be described as "stealth." He's relentless. As he said, "When the guy at the top blocked me, I went to the next level. I would find the two guys out of five who would listen. Together, we developed a war-game process. It was a one-day brainwashing session of role playing to get them to see that other people had strategies that were killing them." Eventually, the virtual reality of the war-gaming experience got the executives to stop denying there were potential problems and instead to focus on what they were going to do about them.

In my own work with companies, I've used a variant of all of these approaches. One of the more interesting was working with Adrienne Johnson Guider of AXA Equitable. We created a senior team off-site in which we role-played how nontraditional competitors could attack the core business. Out of that off-site meeting came several ideas for new forms of collaboration and a greater awareness of the early warnings that all might not be well. The value of this sort of thing, as one executive told me, was that "It wasn't so much that we had the insight that wasn't clear to start with, for those who thought about it. No, the value was that a large set of people who needed to buy in came away with a shared understanding of what we need to be doing."

Fast and Roughly Right Rather Than Precise but Slow

The role of time in a context of temporary arenas is huge. Without the assumption that an advantage will be long-lived, the urgency of an organization to move quickly increases. Slow decision making can be extremely costly. MacMillan and I once did a thought experiment to demonstrate. He's developed a spreadsheet tool called a "BareBones" NPV calculator, which essentially asks people to put numbers around the wave of competitive advantage. Key inputs are how much for launch and for ramp-up, how much return to exploitation, and how long the advantage will last. We then experimented with a new venture one of our clients was attempting to get approved. We found that the six-month delay senior management was proposing for making the decision about whether to go forward dropped total project value by $1.2 million over the life cycle of the project. That's a lot of lost value for management indecision.

The need for speed runs smack into a challenge for corporate governance. Boards of most large organizations are not, by definition, fast-moving creatures. Bill Klepper, one of my colleagues at Columbia, studies boards of directors.[8] I asked him about the timing of board oversight and intervention. He said he thought that if companies were to ask for board intervention more frequently than three times per year, it would dramatically reduce people's willingness to serve on boards. This raises a serious problem: if the competitive rhythm of the marketplace is moving much faster than the rhythm of an organization's governance, then the resulting encumbrance threatens to slow significant decisions to a crawl.

Competing in more granular arenas implies that the right to make strategic decisions needs to be spread much more widely throughout the organization. Action on the front lines is moving so fast that there simply isn't time to get enough rich information back and forth to senior-level decision makers before the opportunity vanishes. This, of course, is what the "emergent and learning" rather than "planning" school of strategy has been saying for years. The dilemma is how one creates strategic coherence when strategy is increasingly distributed across multiple arenas, each of which might have competitive advantages created in somewhat different ways.

My research, and that of many others, suggests that this is where the role of common values and corporate culture comes into play.[9] If one has a common point of view about the right and the wrong things to do, it is much less likely that you will ride off the ranch. Here is the dilemma: The need to build a common culture and framework calls for a sustained interaction between an organization and its people (and other assets). Increasingly, these bonds are becoming frayed. If you believe that strategy making and executing and the capabilities of companies will be identified increasingly with particular individuals, then keeping those people involved and engaged has got to be a huge part of strategy.

Escaping NPV Tyranny: Prototype to Learn

Eric Ries, a successful entrepreneur and author of a smart book called *The Lean Startup*, suggests that you can tell prospective winners from losers not by the quality of their ideas or even by their execution, but rather by their ability to fast-adapt their activities.[10] The secret, he suggests, is a practice he calls "continuous deployment," in which organizations move really fast to uncover the things that aren't working so that they can more quickly get to those things that might. Ryan Jacoby, recently head of the New York studio for IDEO, is a huge proponent of a similar process. "Prototypes," said Ryan in a recent visit to my class, "are made to be broken. The faster you can break it, the more quickly you'll get to a better answer."

The fundamental problem is that when you are trying something new, it isn't typically clear right away which exact configuration of elements is going to be a winner. This suggests that experimentation, trial-and-error learning, and discovery are the key practices. What firms unfortunately often do, however, is try to plan their new businesses as though they were operating with a lot more certainty than they actually are. My colleagues and I have written extensively about this problem in our work on discovery-driven thinking, but it's worth mentioning here: be prepared for a fair amount of iteration at this stage in the process, rather than thinking you can project and anticipate what is going to happen.[11] Ban words such as "projection," "estimate," and "target" from your vocabulary. Replace them with the concepts of "assumption," "feedback," and "check-points" or "milestones." You want to make as many inexpensive, intelligent mistakes as fast as possible while you are still refining the market concept.

Good entrepreneurs typically operate this way. In describing the design of Dr. John's Products' iconic SpinBrush—a toothbrush priced similarly to a manual toothbrush but with the features of far more expensive electric toothbrushes—founder John Osher discusses the fits and starts of the adaptive process, describing how the product went from concept to a bread-board model to a prototype to something that could be tested. Discovering that the bristles on the brush pointed sideways after two weeks of use led him to design them to oscillate rather than rotate—that is the kind of discovery you simply can't make without having a prototype.[12]

Only when you have convinced yourself that you have a winner that the market really wants should you be considering bringing the business up to scale. When that wonderful moment arrives, it makes sense to think about how the offer will evolve in the face of competitive response and user adoption. At Apple, for instance, young designers are expected to mock up how their designs might evolve in a second or third generation. Rather than innovating for a moment, they have a pipeline of innovation ready for subsequent ramp-ups. Luggage maker Tumi follows a similar developmental trajectory, continually refreshing the points of value its products offer by anticipating what business travelers are going to need next. The idea is that having gone to the trouble of developing deep customer insight, you might want to utilize it in developing a series of innovations.

Implications for Talent and Leadership Development: The Learnability Principle

All of this has significant implications for how leaders are identified, trained, developed, and deployed in future organizations. For starters, companies should no longer promote leaders who have only demonstrated capabilities in exploitation situations. Although not everyone will be equally talented at every stage, it is vital that there is enough familiarity with what is needed at each stage to allow the organization to respond effectively at key transition points. Leaders also need to be trained to be constructively paranoid—always looking for evidence of change in their markets and in the state of their advantages, rather than seeking comforting, but misleading, information that makes things look better than they are.

Kris Gopalakrishnan's concept of "learnability," which we introduced in chapter 2, shifts the emphasis in a company's human resources mix from hiring primarily for existing skills to hiring for the ability to acquire new skills. In a world of transient advantage, it isn't always possible to know what kind of people you are going to need, so being able to reconfigure the people that you have can be very helpful.

The scalability of a firm's leadership is likely to be a significant driver of its ability to move from advantage to advantage. This suggests that a significant investment in leadership development will be needed, particularly if organizations seek to retain talented people. In our outlier firms, we clearly saw tremendous investments in making sure that leaders were prepared ahead of the need. The development they receive also helps to reinforce the values that provide strategic coherence even as conditions change. At Infosys, for instance, the philosophy of leadership development is "The company is the campus, business is the curriculum, and leaders teach." Each senior executive regards teaching the next generation of leaders as a personal responsibility.

Nearly over the Cliff: A New Leadership Mind-Set at Alcoa

Part of the reality of the transient-advantage context is that even if they get most of the new strategy playbook right, in an unpredictable and volatile world, companies will sometimes falter. The transition from an old advantage to a new one can be extremely difficult, and firms will often struggle to get it right. The implications are that we should stop judging leaders on whether they had a problem or mistake or not, but rather judge them on how they helped their firms to metaphorically pick themselves up and reignite the next phase of competitive advantage. As I mentioned earlier with respect to CEMEX, it is very frustrating that many of the things a company gets right are overwhelmed in the popular imagination whenever a company has a problem. It's useful, therefore, to see how a firm facing a drastic drop in its core business managed to right itself.

Klaus Kleinfeld is a charismatic (and exhausting) dynamo of a man. I first met him at the Microsoft CEO Summit when he was running the Americas for the German industrial giant Siemens. He and Siemens ended up parting ways, and he landed at aluminum giant Alcoa as president and chief operating officer. He was elected CEO and president the following year, in May of 2008. Who knew what would be waiting for him just a few short months later?

Let's be clear: Alcoa was by no means a slouch in the management department at the time Kleinfeld arrived. CEO Alain Belda was a deeply respected leader, and the CEO who preceded him, Paul O'Neill, has been described as "legendary."[13] The company was on many "best managed" lists and was widely admired for innovations in areas such as safety. Indeed, even when you go into its beautiful Lever House New York offices, about as far from a gritty bauxite mine as you can imagine, you are tagged with a safety tag and shown how to safely navigate the space.

Kleinfeld did not have long to settle into a routine as a newly minted CEO. The global economic downturn sent the price of aluminum into a free-fall practically overnight. He recalled: "When the downturn happened, it was horrible. The price of aluminum on the global exchange dropped more than 50 percent and our customers were canceling orders as demand for their products fell off. The metal price in the summer of 2008 was around $3,200. It dropped to $1,100 by January. In a situation like that it's as if the bottom falls out of your business. There is no way you can adjust your costs fast enough in that kind of time frame. We felt we were really in trouble."

In retrospect, he concluded that the company had been "cruising along with a high price for aluminum" for some time. Kleinfeld saw the precipitous drop as a call to action. He convened his business leaders in a closed-door, two-day emergency session at Alcoa's offices in New York. The first day was dedicated to evaluating the state of the business. And it was not fun. Presentation after presentation detailed the grim facts of customers who were shutting down operations, others who were having difficulties paying their bills, and still others whose growth was at a standstill or reversed in many of Alcoa's end-markets. And, of course, the brutal aluminum price free-fall was sucking all the cash out of Alcoa's operations. Finally, physically and emotionally exhausted, the team called it a night. As Kleinfeld recalls, "People thought we were totally against the wall."

On day two, the stress level was so high that most people could not remain seated in their chairs. Amid a palpable atmosphere of trepidation and anxiety, Kleinfeld describes how he "rolled a white copy board in, closed the doors, and said, 'We're not going to leave until we've worked out a way to survive this cash crisis.'" The team dug in by first figuring out how much cash was needed to get the business through the crisis. Then Kleinfeld, standing in front of the room, marker in hand, moved the discussion from problems to solutions. Ideas began to flow as he wrote all possible cash levers on the board. There could be divestitures. There could be changes made to the way the company worked with suppliers and procured materials. There could be overhead cuts, pay freezes, and curtailments of smelters. Every option was on the table.

Gradually, a way forward began to emerge. By late that evening, the team had identified seven key levers that they would use to restructure and redesign how Alcoa operated. Accountability was key. As Kleinfeld said, "We decided that every member of the leadership team would have an additional role. They have their 'day job,' but in this crisis we can't afford having our top people with just one role. We asked each one to take on a specific lever in what became known as our Cash Sustainability Program. We also assigned emerging leaders to each lever, to give them added opportunities to shine." Somewhat counterintuitively, instead of feeling overwhelmed by the magnitude of what they were up against, the team was "super motivated," according to Kleinfeld. They were energized at the thought that Alcoa had a chance to use the crisis to motivate dramatic change and permanent improvements, to come out stronger than before.

As if this story weren't dramatic enough, there was an unexpected plot twist. To get the last flight home, Kevin Anton, CFO of Alcoa's largest business unit, Global Primary Products, at the time, left the meeting and headed for the airport for a US Airways flight to Charlotte, North Carolina. Three minutes into what had been a perfectly normal flight, the plane stalled after hitting a flock of birds and made what has subsequently been described as a "miracle" landing on the Hudson River thanks to pilot Chesley B. "Sully" Sullenberger, saving the lives of all 155 people aboard. Back at the Alcoa meeting room, the group remaining in the discussion were looking out at the early-setting winter sun when they suddenly got the news that the plane had gone down in the freezing water. As Klaus described it later, "We were all in shock, rushing out of the room, trying to get the news." With the news on the television, Anton phoned in to say that he was OK. The company arranged a plane for him to get back that night to his wife and two boys, who were understandably distraught. Interestingly, Anton later reported that the first thing he thought as the plane descended is that 85 percent of all planes are made of Alcoa aluminum. "I'm really lucky that it is of such high quality!" he observed later.

Nine months later, Anton was finally reunited with his briefcase, which had been left aboard the sinking plane. In the bag was the original copy of the team's handwriting on the white board, stained by water marks from its sojourn in the Hudson. He had it framed, and it decorates the Alcoa offices to this day.

Back at work, the teams revisited ideas that had been previously rejected as too difficult or too radical. For example, one of the essential raw materials used in the electrolysis process to make aluminum in Alcoa's smelting plants is calcined coke. The company had been buying certain high-grade coke, which the suppliers were charging substantially more for than lower grades. Earlier efforts to use lower-grade coke had failed miserably and led to serious instabilities in the production, which the smelter operators had already predicted and then proven. They made their point clear: "Procurement and the technical experts had no idea about the pot room realities."

The crisis forged a new, unlikely, alliance between the field staff and the technical experts with the very real possibility that if the company couldn't get over this crisis, smelters would be shut down. As Kleinfeld says, "This was received by the pot room operators as a very theoretical idea of the procurement team and the so-called technical experts. At the same time they knew that this 'odd idea' —if it really worked—would reduce costs massively and save the plant from curtailments. So under this threat, they embraced it, worked with the experts, and turned it into a big success, setting a new lower cost standard for the operations worldwide." This time the smelter operators demanded to work with the procurement and technical teams and made it happen. Once the first pilot had been successful, Kleinfeld praised the joint team's achievements in his quarterly letter to all 59,000 employees around the world, encouraging all employees to question existing practices, to apply innovations from the company's tech center, and to work in teams to apply those innovations to drive down costs and preserve cash.

The emotional dimension of struggling through devastating setbacks falls heaviest on the CEO. Although every executive will eventually confront dark days, even in the most discouraging times a CEO cannot afford the luxury of showing a lack of confidence. For Kleinfeld, the test came when he realized that he needed to raise cash through an equity offer in the worst period of the economic crisis, when nobody had the guts to raise money. Meeting more than two hundred investors in two grueling days of back-to-back meetings, he admitted, "It was exhausting and a little discouraging because the investors were telling me over and over again that 'We've heard promises from your predecessors before, why should we believe you now?' So when I described the seven levers of the Cash Sustainability Program, I showed our confidence by using their very words, calling them 'Seven Promises' to the company's stakeholders. The result was that we raised $1.4 billion, beating our $1 billion target at a substantially lower cost. With that cash we bought the breathing space that gave us the time to put our programs into effect."

The ultimate success of the Cash Sustainability Program gave the company a lasting advantage over slower and less liquid competitors. As Kleinfeld observes, if you have cash in a downturn, you can take advantage of opportunities that simply don't exist in more stable periods. It also proved to be the catalyst for sweeping, positive changes in how Alcoa manages its business. As of today, the program has exceeded its targets, having saved $2.6 billion in procurement and $509 million in overhead costs; decreased requirements for capital investment; and reduced the amount of money Alcoa has tied up in working capital. After the divestments of low-growth businesses, more than 90 percent of Alcoa's remaining businesses were first or second in their markets.

Reigniting the Growth Engine

Throughout the crisis Alcoa kept its eye on its future, particularly in growth regions. In addition to completing modernization projects in China and Russia, it continued the construction of a mine and refinery in Brazil that had only been 70 percent finished when the economic crisis hit. As the company's cash position improved, it felt strong enough to sign a joint venture in Saudi Arabia to build the lowest-cost integrated aluminum facility in the world. Including a mine, refinery, smelter, and rolling mill, Kleinfeld called the project "a lifetime opportunity to increase Alcoa's competitiveness in every component of our upstream and mid-stream business."

"For us to complete the capital projects in Brazil, Russia, and China was a powerful internal signal that we intended to come out of the crisis stronger than ever," Kleinfeld noted. "Then the Saudi partnership was a major motivational shot in the arm for Alcoa that we had indeed succeeded." As Kleinfeld puts it, "You can't success-fully restructure a company just focusing on cost without always also having growth on the agenda. People only become passionate when they feel part of a great foundation and envision an even brighter future that motivates them to fight through tough times. The very idea of growth is an important emotional dimension for employees as well as for your investors and other stakeholders. That's what gets people through these massive disappointments, and focused on what they *can* influence. It gives them the confi-dence to make difficult decisions without hesitation."

In reflecting on Alcoa's emergence from the tough two-year crisis, one member of the company's management team remarked about the Cash Sustainability Program, "In some pretty rough economic storms, we didn't just keep the boat afloat. We built a different and much stronger boat."

A Different Mind-Set

Clearly, the challenges of fast-moving advantages suggest a different set of organizational assumptions and leadership mind-set than might be appropriate in more stable times. The ability and willingness to seek out actual information, confront bad news, and design appropri-ate responses is critical. Unlike Kodak, the leaders at firms such as Berlitz and Alcoa recognized that even great, long-lived companies need to change their models if they are to thrive. The learnability principle emphasizes continual investment in people, even if one doesn't know exactly what they will be doing. And combating the ten-dency to seek only positive news that confirms existing assumptions is critical.

For most of this book, I've focused on how organizations can be competitive and remain healthy even when particular advantages are transient. A huge, and to my mind still unresolved, set of issues concerns the human impact of all this competition. Our social and economic systems—from the way we allocate health care and retirement obligations to the way we educate people and prepare them for careers—are all imbued with the assumption that organizations are likely to be long-lived and their advantages sustainable. With the advent of a transient-advantage economy, these assumptions will need to be rethought completely. In the next chapter, we'll take a look at what transient advantage means for people.

7

What Transient Advantage Means for You, Personally

For most of this book, I've spent time showing how transient advantages have implications for strategy, for corporate choices, and for how organizations need to operate. In this final chapter, I'd like to shift the focus to what this all means for individual people. In a world of sustainable advantages, you could actually plan a career path and expect a relatively long employment relationship with companies. With transient advantages, as I've said earlier, the metaphor is more like making a movie, putting on the Olympics, or working in a political campaign—the organization itself comes, goes, and changes as competitive needs dictate. The Bureau of Labor Statistics, as I noted in an earlier chapter, has found that companies are using more temporary labor. In some industries, such as retail, the employer/employee

TABLE 7-1

The new strategy playbook: making it personal

From	To
Organizational systems	Individual skills
A stable career path	A series of gigs
Hierarchies and teams	Individual superstars
Infrequent job hunting	Permanent career campaigns
Careers managed by the organization	Careers managed by the individual

relationship has completely turned on its head: where most workers in years past were full-time employees, today most are part-timers with unpredictable hours.[1] The transient-advantage concept has relevance for people, too—just as a company can't cling to an advantage that is becoming obsolete for too long without repercussions, so too individuals can't assume that the skills that were valuable at one time will ensure them a high-quality, productive life thereafter. Let's consider, then, how individuals should be thinking about their prospects in a world of transient advantage (table 7-1).

Competitive Advantage: Power to the People

One somewhat surprising result of transient advantages is that people with the skills and capabilities to help organizations surf successive waves are being rewarded more richly than they ever have before. In previous generations, such individuals would have been groomed and developed from within and would have been less valuable to other organizations (other things being equal) because their talents were embedded in a particular company's operations.

Ironically, the very pressures that led organizations to free themselves from the constraints of owning assets permanently have created a new form of dependency. Firms now put themselves in the position of being beholden to people who have the rare, valuable knowledge, skills, and connections that help to create new advantages. Indeed, for individuals with those capabilities, sustainable competitive advantage at an individual level endures, despite the particular organizational structures it serves at any one point in time.

Fellow strategist Anita McGahan got her start in strategy by looking at industries and how they change.[2] Of late, however, she's been doing some rethinking, even to the point of considering that competitive advantages can only be understood at the individual level. She remarked to me that "there is a floor in a building down in Wall Street, which houses the trust business. They have securities that they are holding in trust. Activities that continue behind this door have not changed in twenty-five years. It's the same people doing the same work, and they have been there with no interruption in the normal course of career progress. At the same time, they have been affiliated with five or six different organizations—the Bank of New York, Citigroup, JPMorgan Chase, and so on." In other words, these people are not dependent on the organization to create the advantages that pay their salaries. Rather, the organizations are dependent on them; otherwise, they can't compete.

Anita suggests that "when you start thinking this way, your view of what competitive advantage is changes. The resources that underlie competitive advantage are increasingly embedded in the relationships between people. People have the knowledge and the embedded relationships and uniquely know how to manage these assets. Those connections are much more persistent than companies that own these resources. They become expert within their community at finding ways to extract value from those resources, sometimes through salaries, stock options, sometimes through compelling M&A deals. We're looking at the wrong level of analysis."

Personal Assets Matter More Than Organizational Ones

Transient advantages mean that certain employees, certain privileged investors, certain contractors, and others benefit from corporate earnings disproportionately from the success of the underlying organization. Moreover, as Anita points out, the "assets" that employees build over their careers are far more durable and valuable than many corporate assets. As is well known in Silicon Valley, employees can change firms with equanimity. "I changed my job without having to change my car pool" is a frequent observation. The individual, in other words, rather than the corporation, is where certain kinds of durable competitive advantages lie, and where they get paid.

Consider this interesting statistic. In assessing the performance of the *Fortune* 500 corporations, the magazine reported that the historical return on sales of this group of large firms in 2010 was 4.7 percent (in 2009 it was 4 percent, up from 1 percent the preceding year).[3] According to the Census Bureau, median pay in the United States was $44,410 per person. So if one takes that as the base sales case to do the calculations, one gets some pretty interesting "return on sale"-type numbers. The average corporate CEO in the United States (which includes CEOs of many small businesses) earned $204,650 in 2010, according to the Census Bureau, a 78.2 percent return. If you compare the total compensation of the average S&P 500 CEO, which the AFL-CIO calculates at $11,358,445, you get a 99.6 percent return.[4] A typical senior partner at a large consulting firm earns over $1 million. A leading business speaker can command $50,000 or more per appearance, and so on. Now, I make no claim that these numbers are all that meaningful, nor do I wish to wade into the debate over CEO compensation.

What is clear, however, is that in non-sustainable-advantage situations, many individuals have the opportunity to do very well indeed, even if the organizations they are affiliated with come and go.

The Old Rules of Personal Success Have Changed

This book started with the argument that the way we think about the concept of strategy needs to change. Where we took for granted in years past that the ultimate goal of strategy was to achieve a sustainable competitive advantage, we really need to be thinking about transient advantage—when individual advantages come and go—rather than believing they will be with us forever, or at least for a long period of time. The best organizational strategies in such an environment are those that promote reconfiguration of the business rather than having drastic layoffs or downsizing. Learning to be competent at disengagement will be important. Mastering the resource allocation process and wresting control away from powerful vested interests within the organization will be significant. Being systematic about innovation will not be optional. The executives and leaders who succeed will bring a different mind-set to their businesses, one that favors candor and is unafraid to confront bad news. The consequences are that the rules for personal success are being rewritten.

For decades, at least in most Western countries, the orthodoxy for success was fairly well accepted. Hard work, investment in education and skills, and commitment to a good employer were generally thought to be the way to get ahead and stay ahead. Similarly, employers took on a somewhat paternalistic role. In addition to offering career progression and development opportunities, the classic benefits of health insurance and defined-benefit pension plans provided buffers against economic uncertainty.

Many of those old-style firms have disappeared or been swallowed up. Those that remain—think IBM, for instance—have totally transformed the way they operate. Risks, such as retirement risk, that used to be borne by companies as legally defined obligations are now carried by individuals. Although unusual companies such as the growth outliers continue to offer lifetime careers and a measure of employment stability, the very fact that they are outliers suggests that this is no longer the norm.

The consequences of these changes for those people pursuing a traditional career path have in many cases been dire. For decades now, one outcome has been the steady rise of income inequality.[5] Although you might think that this would be good news for those in the upper tier, pervasive inequality has actually been associated with slower growth overall and fewer opportunities for everybody, even those doing relatively well.[6] Whole swaths of the Western economies have been hollowed out, as companies grappling with transient advantage find cheaper resources elsewhere. Further, the barriers to competition that created cost buffers that in turn allowed organizations to be relatively benevolent employers have collapsed. Faced with threats from low-cost competitors, companies have been pulling back for years. In a world of transient advantage, the only employees a company will keep are those its leaders believe to be indispensable to its future.

An alternative is to abandon the idea of a more or less linear career path altogether. In ambiguous and uncertain settings, it's not clear what skills are going to be valuable, which connections will matter most, or what the business model in which you'll eventually participate will look like. As the journal *Fast Company* has been exploring, "flux" is increasingly the norm for the careers of more and more people.[7] They will find themselves moving from gig to gig rather than moving up a ladder. More moves will be horizontal. And the organizations that create these opportunities may be temporary themselves.

How Vulnerable Are You?

Just as I would encourage companies to anticipate that their competitive advantages may go into decline, I would encourage people to anticipate this, and to plan their careers accordingly. What this means from a practical point of view is that permanent career management is here to stay. Just as companies need to be investing to discover the next wave of advantage, individuals need to be investing to maintain their skills, stay relevant, and have compelling stories of accomplishment to market their value to others. If you think of yourself as permanently looking for the next job, and prepare accordingly, you are much less likely to be caught by surprise without having done the appropriate amount of homework.

So where do you start considering your own career in light of transient advantage? Let's start with a diagnosis. Complete the self-assessment in table 7-2. If you answered "no" to any of the questions, that's an area of possible vulnerability and a place to consider addressing a weakness. If you answered "no" to five or more of the questions, it's time for immediate action! In the rest of this chapter, I'll walk you through a process for developing your own personal strategy for transient advantage.

If My Current Employer Let Me Go, It Would Be Relatively Easy to Find a Similar Role in Another Organization for Equivalent Compensation

There are two questions you want to be thinking of here. The first is how likely it is that your own organization is going to run into the buzz saw of a fading advantage and that you will be on the losing end of that transformation. (See the sidebar for signals that an existing competitive advantage is under threat or beginning to erode.)

TABLE 7-2

How prepared are you for the transient-advantage economy?

Question	Answer
If my current employer let me go, it would be relatively easy to find a similar role in another organization for equivalent compensation.	Yes/No
If I lost my job today, I am well prepared and know immediately what I would do next.	Yes/No
I've worked in some meaningful capacity (employment, consulting, volunteering, partnering) with at least five different organizations within the last two years.	Yes/No
I've learned a meaningful new skill that I didn't have before in the last two years, whether it is work related or not.	Yes/No
I've attended a course or training program within the last two years, either in person or virtually.	Yes/No
I could name, off the top of my head, at least ten people who would be good leads for new opportunities.	Yes/No
I actively engage with at least two professional or personal networks.	Yes/No
I have enough resources (savings or other) that I could take the time to retrain, work for a small salary, or volunteer in order to get access to a new opportunity.	Yes/No
I can make income from a variety of activities, not just my salary.	Yes/No
I am able to relocate or travel to find new opportunities.	Yes/No

The second is whether the skills you have today are going to be relevant somewhere else, even if your organization can't at the moment utilize them.

If you believe that an advantage in your company is likely to fade away, with negative implications for yourself, you then have two choices. The first is to try to mobilize the powers that be in the organization to tackle sustainable-advantage thinking and begin to put in place the practices that I've described previously in the book. You'll need to convince a critical mass of people that change is necessary and begin to consider how the organization might begin to move toward finding the next-generation advantage. The previous chapters in the book discuss what needs to be done.

Early Warnings of Fading Advantage

The More of These, the Worse Things Are

- I don't buy my own company's products or services.

- We are investing at the same levels or even more and not getting margins or growth in return.

- Customers are finding cheaper or simpler solutions that are "good enough."

- Competition is emerging from places we didn't expect.

- Customers are no longer excited about what we have to offer.

- We are not considered a top place to work by the people we would like to hire.

- Some of our very best people are leaving.

- Our stock is perpetually undervalued.

- Our technical people (scientists and engineers, for instance) are predicting that a new technology will change our business.

- We are not being targeted by headhunters for talent.

- The growth trajectory has slowed or reversed.

- Very few innovations have made it successfully to market in the last two years.

- The company is cutting back on benefits or pushing more risk to employees.

- Management is denying the importance of potential bad news.

Let's say that for whatever reason you don't think it likely that you'll be able to get the organization to change fast enough to adapt, or that powerful people's vested interests make it nearly impossible that change will take place without a major crisis. At that point, it makes sense to prepare yourself to create alternatives. You'll need to do an unflinching audit of where the skills and capabilities you have today may be relevant outside your organization. If you are personally tied to a whole category of activities that are going to disappear, then it's time to make some serious investments in upgrading those skills and seeing where else they might be useful (more on this below).

The advantage of developing an early warning of your organization's being trapped by past competitive advantages is that it can often give you valuable time. That's time you can spend networking, exploring alternatives, building new capabilities, and otherwise making yourself more valuable. The last thing you want is to be surprised. Far too many executives at once-thriving organizations were left behind when competition eroded their advantages.

If I Lost My Job Today, I Am Well Prepared and Know Immediately What I Would Do Next

Being well prepared for an engagement to end means much more than dusting off your résumé. It means being ready to start a permanent campaign for a new and better position (or being willing to start a business or go into consulting). Before you can do that, however, you need to come to grips with the emotional challenge of leaving the past behind—the whole cycle of mourning for what was, which usually includes emotions of sadness, anger, loss, and the like. Give yourself the opportunity to grieve a little—it's only natural.

After pulling yourself together, the next step is to do some strategizing. I'd start with putting together a set of what career consultant

Ford R. Myers calls the "job seekers tool kit."[8] He advises that such a toolkit include the following:

1. A written list of accomplishments

2. A positioning statement

3. A professional biography, which is a one-page narrative of your career in the third person

4. A list of target companies that you would like to work for

5. Your networking lists

6. A set of professional references

7. Letters of recommendation

8. A networking agenda

9. A tracking system

10. Finally, a résumé

As you can see, being prepared to make a move is no small undertaking, but it is critical to be able to shift your career even as the underlying businesses you are working in change. There are many excellent resources, including Myers's website, that can help with the details of how to prepare yourself for a career transition.

The other point to remember, particularly in those early mournful days when the bad news is first presented, is that almost everyone who ended up being very successful has had setbacks, been fired, or otherwise run into a rough patch. J. K. Rowling lost her job as a secretary for Amnesty International because instead of focusing on secretarial work, she daydreamed about a world of wizards. Her severance pay provided the resources on which she supported herself while writing the fabulously successful *Harry Potter* series.

Michael Bloomberg was fired from Salomon Brothers in a political dustup and went on to found Bloomberg, which grew into a media empire. He became a billionaire and a three-term mayor of New York City. Salomon Brothers? It no longer exists. *Vogue* editor Anna Wintour was fired from her first job in fashion for being "too edgy." A Baltimore TV producer pulled Oprah Winfrey from a slot anchoring the evening news, proclaiming that she was "unfit" for the job.[9] And so it goes—it is virtually impossible to tell in advance where you are going to end up, so the best thing to do is learn from past experiences and prepare for what comes next.

I've Worked in Some Meaningful Capacity (Employment, Consulting, Volunteering, Partnering) with at Least Five Different Organizations within the Last Two Years

Since careers today are unlikely to be spent within the confines of one organization, having contact with and connections with multiple types of organizations can give you a lot more options. As *Fast Company* reports in its "generation flux" article, a great many people have reworked the idea of what a career is in the first place. Instead of a progression in which deeper and deeper skills are developed along a given trajectory, people work instead on gigs, each one of which might be relatively short but which give them skills, network contacts, and capabilities that can enrich the next engagement and which in turn make them more valuable to the next employer.

Having exposure to a number of different organizational environments is helpful in a transient-advantage economy because it broadens the number of opportunities you might find. Consider the fascinating career path of Japan's Masayoshi Son, currently a part owner of Softbank, which has big stakes in one of our outlier companies, Yahoo! Japan. He was born to an ethnically Korean family on an out-of-the-way island of Japan. His father was a pig farmer who sold illegal alcohol on the side and eventually went into the pachinko parlor business. He decided, according to the *Wall Street Journal*, that his chances as an ethnic minority in Japan were not good and persuaded his parents to allow him to attend high school in the United States. He eventually attended the University of California at Berkeley. He started his entrepreneurial career while there, with an initial product that he talked one of his professors into designing, then licensed it to Sharp Electronics for $500,000. He went into the video-arcade business and several other ventures, some of which never got off the ground, before returning to Japan to found Softbank, initially a software distribution company, in 1981. This was followed by interests in a variety of internet companies, the Comdex computer show, Ziff-Davis Publishing, and Yahoo! Inc. China's Alibaba also was an investment target for Son. With the bursting of the dot-com bubble, Softbank's market value in 2002 was off 98 percent from its earlier peak, and Son took a beating in terms of his own personal wealth. He eventually moved into telecommunications, first with broadband and later with mobile phones. Today, he is proposing to do a deal with Sprint that has the potential to destabilize competition in the wireless market in the United States.[10] Although his career is certainly unusual in both its entrepreneurialism and his later success, the principle of making sure you have exposure to a number of different organizational settings could apply to anyone.

In the Last Two Years I've Learned a Meaningful New Skill That I Didn't Have Before, Whether It Is Work Related or Not

One clear implication of the transient-advantage economy is that a lifelong accumulation of new skills is imperative. Another is that you simply never know when a particular skill will turn out to be valuable, even if you didn't acquire it ostensibly for business. Steve

Jobs of Apple fame liked to tell the story of how he audited a class in calligraphy at his university. Calligraphy didn't have much to do with technology, but later on, Jobs's understanding of calligraphy influenced the way computer characters on WYSIWYG screens would look. That's a great example of a skill or bit of knowledge that one didn't know in advance would come in handy but that eventually paid off in an unexpected way.

Rare skills can also be significant differentiators. I was talking to one of my participants at a Columbia executive education class as he described the difficulty his firm (a pharmaceutical company) was having penetrating certain markets in China. "In the end," he said, "do you know who the most highly paid salesperson in our entire global company is?" I said I didn't. "It's the guy who is not only a great salesman but also has great English!"

New skills can be gained by formal training, of course, but it is also worthwhile to think of contexts you might work in that could offer some ways to build skills that are a little untraditional. Volunteering and working on community projects are often great ways to practice doing new things. The key thing you want to push yourself to do is to keep adding skills—tools, if you will—to your personal toolbox. You never know when they might come in handy.

One of the most exciting new areas in the skill-building arena are the free, online courses offered by organizations such as the Khan Academy. The academy famously began in 2004 when a Bangladeshi-American named Salman Khan, with degrees from MIT and Harvard Business School, was asked by his cousin Nadia to give her some math help. He began tutoring her using drawings done with Yahoo's Doodle notepad. Other relatives asked for help, and Khan posted the lessons to YouTube. The idea took off, and in 2009 Khan quit his job in finance as a hedge fund analyst for Connective Capital Management to focus on the tutorials. Today, the academy offers bite-sized video lessons on a breathtaking number of subjects, together with many ancillary offerings such as scoring and keeping track of progress. Among the impacts the academy has had is to reverse the traditional method of teaching. In traditional teaching, teachers deliver the lesson, and students do homework at night to reinforce it. With Khan Academy tutorials available, students do the lesson at night and then practice putting the material into use the next day, with the teacher's help. It's a completely new way of teaching and learning. As of this writing, there are over 3,600 tutorials available. They are free, and they take ten to fifteen minutes. Why not spend some time learning a new skill?

I've Attended a Course or Training Program within the Last Two Years, Either in Person or Virtually

To me, one of the most exciting developments in the transient-advantage context is that education has become far more accessible, democratized, and personal than it has ever been before. With the advent of digitization and brand-new forms of learning, just about anyone with an internet connection can enhance their skills and understanding dramatically. This is going to reshape the education business in new and significant ways.

Executive education

One of the best parts of my job at Columbia Business School is that I am regularly in the role of designing or teaching in our executive education programs. These are mostly short (a week or less) non-degree-granting programs whose goal is to synthesize the very best of management thinking and share it with practicing executives. For the executives who attend, the programs are a rare opportunity to take a break from the rush of normal business, meet with people from other industries, create new networking opportunities, and, most important, gain some perspective. It's been interesting to me to observe how our executive education classrooms have changed, since I joined Columbia's faculty in 1993, to reflect the changing needs of executives in the transient-advantage economy.

Executive education courses used to be a lot like conventional classroom experiences—professors would get up and give inspiring lectures or lead vibrant case discussions, and that was about it. Today, although we still do some of that, many more elements have been added to the mix. In Columbia Business School's flagship senior executive program (CSEP), for instance, coaching and feedback figure prominently throughout the design, with input from faculty, professional executive coaches, and peers from other industries and sectors. Participants are guided through the development of a personal leadership statement—which they practice—and helped to resolve a personal case involving a strategic issue they are struggling with. Highly interactive sessions are supplemented by opportunities for peer-to-peer team leadership. In that course, a segment entitled "Executive Well-Being" is included to help people focus on their health. Competing in a transient-advantage world is stressful and can take a toll on people, physically.

The senior executive program is four weeks long, so it is quite a commitment. The rewards, however, can be substantial. Marco Mattiacci, a senior executive with Ferrari of North America, made the decision to join in 2011, saying, "It is a great opportunity at this stage of my career to stop for a few weeks and fine-tune, update my knowledge, plus have the opportunity to confront myself with other colleagues from different industries and bring new ideas coming from different areas of business." It must have worked pretty well— Marco received the Automotive Executive of the Year award in February of 2012. The release announcing his award credited him with growing sales in his areas by 20 percent, allowing Ferrari to hold a top position in the exclusive automobile segment. He in turn

Creating a Learning Community in the Columbia Senior Executive Program

Executive education was once focused mostly on the content of the courses, and the model was very much professor-driven. Today's best programs have changed this model entirely, with a far greater focus on process and values and learning driven largely in a peer-to-peer manner, with professors taking the role of facilitators within a learning community. In CSEP, a considerable amount of time is spent on creating this learning community, beginning before the participants arrive—with telephone interviews, exercises as the participants come together for the first time, and explicit structuring of the values that the CSEP community chooses to work on together. In a recent class, the following values were selected by the community: 1) Encourage your colleagues, 2) Optimistic listening, 3) Have fun, 4) Trust and respect others, and 5) Take personal responsibility for the success of every session at CSEP. Participants work throughout the course with a "learning journal," which facilitates deep reflection and the capture of core ideas. Participants are also encouraged to take the time they spend at the course to refresh themselves emotionally and physically and to build and maintain peer networks that can continue long after the end of the course.

credits what he learned at CSEP with helping him achieve these results. Oh, and I should mention that while I do teach in CSEP I am not the faculty director—credit for its innovative design really belongs to Paul Ingram, Bruce Craven, and to Schon Beechler, who preceded them.

I do direct a shorter, one-week program on leading change and growth, in which a key element of the program design is the application of all the concepts and frameworks to a real-life personal case, which serves to both reinforce what people are learning and to help them make progress on an issue involving growth or change that they are concerned about. As one of my participants, the director of strategy and business development for Philips Electronics Middle East and Africa, told me, "One year after LSGC [Leading Strategic Growth and Change], an enduring lesson in our organization is that our growth strategy is nothing more than the initiatives you drive and how you manage them . . . For us, LSGC translated into a system to manage initiatives for growth: with more discipline, more granularity, better assumptions tracking, clearer consequences, and therefore stronger internal commitment (i.e., funding via the yearly budget cycle) to pursue growth." As I said, today's executive education courses are moving toward real-world application much more aggressively than they did in the past.

Other educational experiences

Executive education is not for everyone. There are, however, many other options for continuing your own development and investing in your capabilities. I mentioned the Khan Academy previously. Community colleges, local arts organizations, vocational schools, and other institutions are also places to pick up new skills.

Entrepreneurs everywhere have started to develop learning that can be delivered in a variety of ways, some of it very cost effectively. University Now, for instance, is a social venture based in San Francisco whose mission is "Making higher education available for everyone by building the most affordable and accessible universities in the world." Gene Wade, the cofounder and CEO, felt that traditional systems of education were failing far too many people, and he launched the organization to address these flaws. In particular, University Now makes higher education, whose cost has become prohibitive for far too many people, affordable.

What Should You Look for in an Executive Education Program? An Opinionated List

- A dedicated faculty director or designer who is on-site throughout your learning experience

- The opportunity to apply what you are learning to your own situation

- A diverse mix of participants from different countries, regions, and industries

- An appropriate level of participant experience (you don't want a huge disparity in experience levels)

- An up-to-date curriculum with current examples

- Appropriate use of technology to support your learning (web pages, apps, etc.)

- Help in getting prepared for the course and in following up afterward

- A mix of learning styles in the content—some action oriented, some more reflective, some designed with a specific goal in mind

- Enough downtime to reflect and apply new knowledge

- Diversity in the faculty presenting

- Experience of the institution offering the course (there is a pretty steep learning curve)

With the advent of massively open online courses (MOOCs) being pioneered by universities such as Stanford and MIT, online education is going to become an affordable reality for an increasingly large number of people.

I Could Name, Off the Top of My Head, at Least Ten People Who Would Be Good Leads for New Opportunities

In a transient-advantage economy, one of the few things that will endure are relationships. Access to a network is one of the most powerful ways in which people can maintain their value to others, find new opportunities, and create opportunities for others in exchange. Indeed, the growth outliers put a huge emphasis on the stability of their relationships with employees and with customers. FactSet boasts that its client retention rate has been 95 percent over the past ten years. Analysts observe that both Infosys and Cognizant have strong client retention (with Cognizant boasting of a 90 percent client satisfaction rate on a recent survey, and Infosys reporting retention of 95 percent in a recent interview with us). Indra Sistemas observes in its annual report that "Indra considers its suppliers and knowledge institutions to be partners in value creation and allies in innovation, and that is a major responsibility."

Smart companies also realize that when layoffs or firings are necessary, it is still important to husband the networks to which these people are tied. Nancy McKinstry, the CEO of publisher Wolters Kluwer, has had to confront this problem as the company makes a difficult transition to a digital world. I asked her how she deals with the people side of transitions. Interestingly, the company has a well-thought-out and conscious process for doing this. A team of people examines options for redeploying the staff elsewhere in the organization as the first choice. McKinstry reports that they have been mostly successful in this regard.

Rudy Lobo, COO of the temporary office company Regus, is clear that parting ways in a reasonably friendly manner is important both to the individual being released and the company as a whole. He describes how it typically might proceed. "Well," he said, "at first people go through a whole irrational phase. They get the news, they get angry, and eventually they calm down. I go through a whole process of bringing them with me. I talk to the husbands, the wives, and try to talk them out of the 30 percent of the bad advice they get . . . I try to set it up so that we part friends."

I Actively Engage with at Least Two Professional or Personal Networks

Relationships are important at work, but other types of network ties matter as well. You've heard it a thousand times from career self-help books, so I won't belabor it here, but it does bear a short reminder: join in. Join alumni groups, neighborhood groups, the chamber of commerce, a book club—any place where you might meet people who could bring you news of an opportunity.

Lately, a new trend is for a network to seek you out because your participation adds value. Social networks, such as Facebook, become more valuable as more people use them. Advice sites, review sites, sites for sharing expertise—these are all places to engage in some networking behavior because it adds value for everyone else.

I Have Enough Resources (Savings or Other) That I Could Take the Time to Retrain, Work for a Small Salary, or Volunteer in Order to Get Access to a New Opportunity

The reality of a transient-advantage economy is that you will sometimes find you'll need to invest in yourself before you can make the next move, and that is going to require resources. Therefore, one of the general principles of competing in this way is that you need to create that buffer capacity so that you don't get stuck in a place that is unattractive, or find that you can't make the next leap you would like to because of constrained resources.

Part of the skill of doing this is to always be thinking of creating spare capacity. Barter instead of buy, keep expenses variable, and try to limit the burden of your operating costs as much as you can. The fewer other obligations, such as debts or fixed commitments you have, the easier it will be to conserve resources. Sometimes you can approach transitions with the support of a partner. In my own case, a difficult but ultimately satisfying transition from running an information technology group for a government agency to spending four years in a PhD program was only possible because my husband was willing to both give up my income and pay for day care during that time.

I Can Make Income from a Variety of Activities, Not Just My Salary

One of the big new developments in a transient-advantage world is that today it is entirely possible to generate multiple income streams beyond simply earning a salary. The more you are able to tap into these, the less vulnerable you are to a shift in that underlying job.

You can be a virtual assistant and sell your administrative capabilities part-time. You can take over jobs other people would like to outsource (and you can outsource everything these days, from menu planning to putting together a one-year-old's birthday party). You can sell things for other people on eBay once you've exhausted the contents of your own closets. You can design apps with handy-to-use developer tools. You can do "tasks" on Amazon's Mechanical Turk system. You can teach. You can consult.

Markets are also emerging in which providers will actually pay you to participate. Skilled gamers, for instance, can be hired by others to play, sometimes converting virtual currency into real currency. You can be paid to provide an opinion or to provide an endorsement.

I Am Able to Relocate or Travel to Find Another Opportunity, if Necessary

Opportunities, unfortunately, may pop up in arenas that are not located near you. It is helpful, therefore, if you have some flexibility about either relocating entirely or being prepared to travel to where the opportunities are. As I interact with executives, I am often struck by how many of them lead peripatetic lives. Living in one place with an office in one or more different locations—often a plane ride away—has become quite normal.

Rudy Lobo, who, as I mentioned, is the chief operating officer of the Regus Group, is representative of this breed. He's a man in a permanent hurry. Intense and energetic, he tells me that he is finally considering establishing a permanent home in a semirural part of England after "thirty moves in thirty years." All that momentum is not accidental. Lobo's company "gets" transient advantage. It was founded in 1989 by Mark Dixon, a colorful serial entrepreneur from the United Kingdom who had run a sandwich business, sold hot dogs from a van, and ventured into bread baking before he had his "aha" moment about a major gap in the market. Sitting in a café in Brussels, where he landed after having already had quite an eventful career with many ups and downs, he had a moment of inspiration. All around him were businesspeople awkwardly taking notes and trying to work amidst shoppers, students, and house-wives, because they were not near their offices. At that time, if you were working and on the road, the local coffee shop or diner was about your only option for a meeting. The idea for a business center that could be rented on an as-needed basis was born.

Since then, Regus has both benefited from and exemplified strategy when competitive advantages are short. Today, it is present in 95 countries, with facilities in 550 cities. It's listed on the London Stock Exchange and is a constituent of the FTSE 250. It's had a turbulent history, with setbacks in the dot-com era and again in the early 2000s, but nonetheless has shown a steady growth trajectory, expanding both its geographic footprint and its services. Today, it offers a vast number of services, from disaster recovery to virtual offices. It moves into and out of geographies and businesses with rhythmic regularity.

Living in the Transient-Advantage Economy

This book began with the premise that strategy, at least as it has been practiced for some time, is stuck. Stuck in ways of thinking that may have made a lot of sense when industries were stable, when trends were more or less predictable, and when the pace of technological evolution seemed to be slower. The idea of strategy then was to achieve stability via a sustainable competitive advantage.

Today, that way of thinking about strategy is in tatters. It would be easy to bemoan the loss of so much security and stability, and it is indeed important to be candid about the downsides and the social adjustment costs. But I think it's just as important to be excited about the opportunities so much dynamism in our economy creates. There will be more room for people to be entrepreneurial. There will be much more variety in how we cobble together our careers, meaning there will be many more on-ramps for people who need to step away for a while. There will be a need, yes, but also tremendous opportunities for more people to obtain the skills and education they will need to be effective in the transient-advantage economy.

Like it or not, the transient-advantage economy is here with us now and shows no sign of retreat. My hope is that in reading this book and learning about the extraordinary people and organizations who have figured out how to thrive in this new landscape, you will be inspired and excited.

Notes

Preface

1. W. Kiechel, *The Lords of Strategy: The Secret Intellectual History of the New Corporate World* (Boston: Harvard Business Press, 2010); B. D. Henderson, "The Experience Curve Revisited," *bcg.perspectives* 229, 1980; M. Porter, *Competitive Advantage: Creating and Sustaining Superior Performance* (New York: The Free Press, 1985).

2. R. G. McGrath and I. C. MacMillan, *The Entrepreneurial Mindset: Strategies for Continuously Creating Opportunity in an Age of Uncertainty* (Boston: Harvard Business School Press, 2000), xv, 380; R. G. McGrath and I. C. MacMillan, *MarketBusters: 40 Strategic Moves That Drive Exceptional Business Growth* (Boston: Harvard Business School Press, 2005); R. G. McGrath and I. C. MacMillan, *Discovery-Driven Growth: A Breakthrough Process to Reduce Risk and Seize Opportunity* (Boston: Harvard Business Press, 2009).

3. R. A. Burgelman, "A Process Model of Internal Corporate Venturing in the Diversified Major Firm," *Administrative Science Quarterly* 18, no. 2 (1983): 223–244; K. Eisenhardt and B. Tabrizi, "Accelerating Adaptive Processes: Product Innovation in the Global Computer Industry," *Administrative Science Quarterly* 40, no. 1 (1995): 84–110; Z. Block and I. C. MacMillan, *Corporate Venturing: Creating New Businesses within the Firm* (Boston: Harvard Business School Press, 1993), x, 371.

4. R. G. McGrath and I. C. MacMillan, "Discovery-Driven Planning," *Harvard Business Review*, July 1995, 44–54.

5. D. Rigby, "Management Tools and Techniques: A Survey," *California Management Review*, January 2001, 139–160.

6. A. Humphrey, "SWOT Analysis for Management Consulting," *SRI Alumni Newsletter*, December 2005.

7. I. C. MacMillan, "Seizing Competitive Initiative," *Journal of Business Strategy* 2, no. 4 (1982): 43.

8. R. A. D'Aveni and R. E. Gunther, *Hypercompetition: Managing the Dynamics of Strategic Maneuvering* (New York: The Free Press, 1994); I. C. MacMillan, "Controlling Competitive Dynamics by Taking Strategic Initiative," *Academy of Management Executive* 2, no. 2 (1988): 111–118.

9. M. Boisot, *Information Space: A Framework for Learning in Organizations, Institutions and Culture* (London: Routledge, 1995).

10. C. M. Christensen, *The Innovator's Dilemma: When New Technologies Cause Great Firms to Fail* (Boston: Harvard Business School Press, 1997), xxiv, 225.

11. S. D. Anthony, *The Little Black Book of Innovation: How it Works, How to Do It* (Boston: Harvard Business Review Press, 2011).

12. R. G. McGrath, "A Real Options Logic for Initiating Technology Positioning Investments," *Academy of Management Review* 22, no. 4 (1997): 974–996.

13. R. G. McGrath, "Falling Forward: Real Options Reasoning and Entrepreneurial Failure," *Academy of Management Review* 24, no. 1 (1999): 13–30; R. G. McGrath, "Failing by Design," *Harvard Business Review*, April 2011, 76–83; R. Gunther and K. Thomas, "The Value Captor's Process: Getting the Most out of Your New Business Ventures," *Harvard Business Review*, May 2007, 128.

14. McGrath and MacMillan, *MarketBusters*.

15. C. MacMillan and R. G. McGrath, "Crafting R&D Project Portfolios," *Research-Technology Management* 45, no. 5 (2002): 48–59.

16. Anthony, *The Little Black Book of Innovation*; A. Ulwick, "Do You Really Know What Your Customers Are Trying to Get Done?" *Strategy and Innovation*, March 2003; I. C. MacMillan and R. McGrath, "Discovering New Points of Differentiation," *Harvard Business Review*, July–August 1997, 133–145.

17. R. G. McGrath, "Finding Opportunities in Business Model Innovation," *European Financial Review*, June–July 2011, 14–17; R. McGrath, "Business Models: A Discovery Driven Approach," *Long Range Planning*, April–May 2010, 247.

18. R. G. McGrath, I. C. MacMillan, and M. L. Tushman, "The Role of Executive Team Actions in Shaping Dominant Designs: Towards the Strategic Shaping of Technological Progress," *Strategic Management Journal* 13, issue S2 (1992): 137–161; I. C. MacMillan and R. G. McGrath, "Nine New Roles for Technology Managers," *Research-Technology Management* 47, no. 3 (2004): 16–26; R. G. McGrath, "The Misunderstood Role of the Middle Manager in Driving Successful Growth Programs," in *The Search for Organic Growth*, ed. E. D. Hess and R. K. Kazanjian (Cambridge, England: Cambridge University Press, 2006), 147–171; R. G. McGrath, "Early Warnings of a Pending Disruption in an Existing Business Model: A Leader's Responsibility," in *The 2009 Pfeiffer Annual Leadership Development*, ed. D. Dotlich et al. (San Francisco: John Wiley & Sons), 264–276.

Chapter 1

1. B. Trumbore, "The Hunt Brothers and the Silver Bubble," BUYand-HOLD, 2012, http://www.buyandhold.com/bh/en/education/history/2000/hunt_bros.html.

2. S. McGee, "The Index's Dark Days in 1980," *Wall Street Journal*, 1996.

3. L. M. Fuld, *The Secret Language of Competitive Intelligence: How to See Through and Stay Ahead of Business Disruptions, Distortions, Rumors, and Smoke Screens* (New York: Crown Business, 2006).

4. I. M. Kunii, G. Smith, and N. Gross, "Fuji: Beyond Film," *Business-Week*, November 21, 1999, 132–138.

5. L. Fuld, "How to Anticipate Wrenching Change," *Chief Executive*, August 1, 2004.

6. S. Hori, "Fixing Japan's White Collar Economy: A Personal View," *Harvard Business Review*, November–December 1993, 157–172.

7. K. Inagaka and J. Osawa, "Fujifilm Thrived by Changing Focus," *Wall Street Journal*, January 20, 2012.

8. Hoover's Inc., *Fujifilm Holdings Full Report Company Profile*, 2012.

9. W. Dabrowski, "Update 1—RIM Co-CEO Doesn't See Threat from Apple's iPhone," Reuters, February 12, 2007.

10. A. Troianovski, "Cellphones Are Eating the Family Budget," *Wall Street Journal*, September 28, 2012.

11. World Bank, "World Development Indicators and Global Development Finance," World DataBank, 2012.

12. M. F. Guillén and E. García-Canal, *The New Multinationals: Spanish Firms in a Global Context* (New York: Cambridge University Press, 2010).

13. V. Mahanta, "How Aditya Puri Has Managed to Pull Off 30% Plus Growth for HDFC Bank," *Economic Times*, June 29, 2012.

14. S. Srinivasan and K. Vasanth, "'Giving Back to Society Is What You Are About': Francisco D'Souza, CEO, Cognizant," *Outlook India*, 2012, http://business.outlookindia.com/print.aspx?articleid=470&editionid=18&ca-tgid=13&subcatgid=26.

15. Mahanta, "How Aditya Puri Has Managed to Pull Off 30% Plus Growth for HDFC Bank."

Chapter 2

1. D. Searcey, K. B. Dennis, and A. Latour, "Verizon to Shed Phone-Book Unit; A Deal That Could Exceed $17 Billion Reflects Shift in Focus to TV, Internet," *Wall Street Journal*, December 5, 2005, A3.

2. FundingUniverse, "Milliken & Co. History," www.fundinguniverse.com/company-histories/milliken-co-history/.

3. T. J. Minchin, "Us Is Spelled U.S.: The Crafted with Pride Campaign and the Fight Against Deindustrialization in the Textile and Apparel Industry," *Labor History* 53, no. 1 (2012): 1–23.

4. J. Bussey, "The Anti-Kodak: How a U.S. Firm Innovates and Thrives," *Wall Street Journal*, January 13, 2012.

5. G. Beaubien, "Now Playing: Netflix Consumer Backlash," *Public Relations Tactics* 18, no. 10 (2011): 4.

6. Grupo ACS, "Corporate Strategy," www.grupoacs.com/index.php/en/c/aboutacs_corporatestrategy.

7. A. Mehta, "A Report on Organizational Behaviour of HDFC Bank," July 7, 2009, www.scribd.com/doc/17163923/A-Report-on-Organizational-BEHAVIOUR-of-HDFC-Bank.

8. Senn-Delaney Leadership Consulting Group, "Interview with Atmos Energy CEO Bob Best," www.senndelaney.com/bobbestarticle.html.

9. Seeking Alpha, "FactSet Research Systems CEO Discusses F4Q 2011 Results—Earnings Call Transcript," September 20, 2011, seekingalpha.com/article/294798-factset-research-systems-ceo-discusses-f4q-2011-results-earnings-call-transcript.

10. Y. Nan, "Buying a Better Brew: Chinese Top Brewer's New Business Pattern Under Low Carbon Economy," *ChinAfrica*, November 2010, www.chinafrica.cn/english/company_profile/txt/2010-10/27/content_306815_2.htm.

11. V. Mahanta, "How Aditya Puri Has Managed to Pull Off 30% Plus Growth for HDFC Bank," *Economic Times*, June 29, 2012.

Chapter 3

1. "RIM Thought iPhone Was Impossible in 2007," Electronista, December 27, 2010, www.electronista.com/articles/10/12/27/rim.thought.apple.was.lying.on.iphone.in.2007/.

2. P. Nunes and T. Breene, *Jumping the S-Curve: How to Beat the Growth Cycle, Get on Top, and Stay There* (Boston: Harvard Business Review Press, 2011).

3. A. G. Lafley, "What Only the CEO Can Do," *Harvard Business Review*, May 2009, 54–62.

4. R. Foster and S. Kaplan, *Creative Destruction: Why Companies That Are Built to Last Underperform the Market—and How to Successfully Transform Them* (New York: Doubleday, 2011).

5. L. Dranikoff, T. Koller, and A. Schneider, "Divestiture: Strategy's Missing Link," *Harvard Business Review*, May 2002, 75–83.

6. C. Matlack, "Norway's Schibsted: No. 3 in Online Classifieds," *Bloomberg BusinessWeek*, October 14, 2010.

7. C. Goff, "Putting the 'New' Back into Newspapers," *Financial Times*, February 8, 2005.

8. "Compared to Schibsted's CEO [in Swedish]," NA24 Propaganda, February 10, 2010, www.na24.no/propaganda/article2534696.ece.

9. K. Lowe, "Kjell Aamot: Johnston Press' New, Controversial Non-Executive Director," July 21, 2010, http://kristinelowe.blogs.com/kristine_lowe/2010/07/kjell-aamot-johnston-press-new-controversial-nonexecutive-director-.html.

10. R. G. McGrath, K. Thomas, and T. Taina, "Extracting Value from Corporate Venturing," *MIT Sloan Management Review* 48, no. 1 (2006): 50.

11. P. Burrows, "Nokia's Epic Fail: Stephen Elop's Nokia Adventure," *BusinessWeek*, June 3, 2011.

12. Ibid.

13. S. Rosenbush, et al., "Verizon's Gutsy Bet," *BusinessWeek*, August 4, 2003, 52–62.

14. D. Searcey, K. B. Dennis, and A. Latour, "Verizon to Shed Phone-Book Unit; A Deal That Could Exceed $17 Billion Reflects Shift in Focus to TV, Internet," *Wall Street Journal*, December 5, 2005, A3.

15. S. Ward, "You Can Really Hear Them Now," *Barron's*, February 2, 2009, 24.

16. A. Thomson, "Losses Put Cemex Under Pressure," *Financial Times*, October 26, 2011, 17.

17. Ibid.

18. S. Crista, "Obsolete Products Fuel a Cottage Industry," *EBN*, June 16, 2003, 4.

19. D. S. Nelson, "Emperor of Steel," *Fortune*, July 12, 2006, 100.

Chapter 4

1. J. L. Bower, *Managing the Resource Allocation Process: A Study of Corporate Planning and Investment* (Boston: Division of Research, Graduate School of Business Administration, Harvard University, 1970), xv, 363; J. Pfeffer and G. Salancik, *The External Control of Organizations: A Resource Dependence Perspective* (Stanford, CA: Stanford University Press, 1978).

2. F. Rose, "The Civil War Inside Sony," *Wired*, February 2003.

3. R. G. McGrath and I. C. MacMillan, *MarketBusters: 40 Strategic Moves That Drive Exceptional Business Growth* (Boston: Harvard Business School Press, 2005).

4. P. Burrows and J. Greene, "Yes, Steve, You Fixed It. Congrats! Now What's Act Two?" *BusinessWeek*, July 31, 2000.

5. "CAT, TOT Near 3G Pact," *Bangkok Post*, June 26, 2011.

6. R. Cooper, "Leadership Development Program: Knowledge-Intensive Growth at DuPont," *Wharton Leadership Digest*, July 2000.

7. S. D. Anderson, "Elevate," *Fast Company*, December 2008–January 2009, 46.

8. J. Neff, "TerraCycle Inc. Builds an Empire on a Foundation Made of Compost," *Waste & Recycling News*, January 23, 2012, 20.

9. A. Aston, "Now, That's Really a Turf War," *BusinessWeek*, April 23, 2007, 12.

10. T. Szaky, *Revolution in a Bottle* (New York: Portfolio, 2009); S. Taylor, "Worm Poop Barons Avoid a Legal Mess," *Maclean's*, October 22, 2007, 44.

11. Szaky, *Revolution in a Bottle*, xviii.

12. D. Roberts, "Under Armour Gets Serious," *Fortune*, October 26, 2011.

13. M. Rich, "Weighing Costs, Companies Favor Temporary Help," *New York Times*, December 19, 2010.

Chapter 5

1. S. D. Anthony, *The Little Black Book of Innovation: How It Works, How to Do It* (Boston: Harvard Business Review Press, 2011); Z. Block and I. C. MacMillan, *Corporate Venturing: Creating New Businesses within the Firm* (Boston: Harvard Business School Press, 1993), x, 371; C. M. Christensen, S. D. Anthony, and E. A. Roth, *Seeing What's Next: Using the Theories of Innovation to Predict Industry Change* (Boston: Harvard Business School Press, 2004), xxxix, 312; G. C. O'Connor, *Grabbing Lightning: Building a Capability for Breakthrough Innovation* (New York: Jossey-Bass, 2008).

2. R. Burgelman and L. Valikangas, "Managing Internal Corporate Venturing Cycles," *Sloan Management Review*, July 2005, 26–34.

3. S. D. Anthony, *The Silver Lining: An Innovation Playbook for Uncertain Times* (Boston: Harvard Business School Press, 2009); C. M. Christensen and M. E. Raynor, *The Innovator's Solution: Creating and Sustaining Successful Growth* (Boston: Harvard Business School Press, 2003), x, 304.

4. S. M. Shapiro, *Best Practices Are Stupid: 40 Ways to Out-Innovate the Competition* (New York: Portfolio/Penguin, 2011).

5. L. A. Bettencourt and A. W. Ulwick, "The Customer-Centered Innovation Map," *Harvard Business Review*, May 2008, 109–114.

6. B. Brown and S. D. Anthony, "How P&G Tripled Its Innovation Success Rate," *Harvard Business Review*, June 2011, 64–72.

7. R. G. McGrath and I. C. MacMillan, *The Entrepreneurial Mindset: Strategies for Continuously Creating Opportunity in an Age of Uncertainty* (Boston: Harvard Business School Press, 2000), xv, 380.

8. R. G. McGrath and I. C. MacMillan, *Discovery-Driven Growth: A Breakthrough Process to Reduce Risk and Seize Opportunity* (Boston: Harvard Business Press, 2009).

9. Christensen and Raynor, *The Innovator's Solution*, x, 304.

10. N. S. Vageesh, "HDFC Bank, Vodafone India Launch Mobile Banking Product for Rural Coverage," *Hindu Business Line*, November 27, 2011.

11. N. S. Ramnath, "How Cognizant Overtook Infosys," *Forbes India*, August 7, 2012.

12. G. C. O'Connor, A. Corbett, and R. Pierantozzi, "Create Three Distinct Career Paths for Innovators," *Harvard Business Review*, December 2009, 78–79.

13. McGrath and MacMillan, *Discovery-Driven Growth*.

14. Brown and Anthony, "How P&G Tripled Its Innovation Success Rate."

15. S. Adhikari, "Brambles Waits to Exhale," *Business Spectator*, February 17, 2010.

16. Macquarie Digital, "Brambles Limited: CEO Interview with Tom Gorman," October 8, 2012.

17. Block and MacMillan, *Corporate Venturing*; A. B. van Putten and I. C. MacMillan, *Unlocking Opportunities for Growth: How to Profit from Uncertainty While Limiting Your Risk* (Upper Saddle River, NJ: Wharton School Publishing, 2009); R. G. McGrath and I. C. MacMillan, "MarketBusting: Strategies for Exceptional Business Growth," *Harvard Business Review*, March 2005, 80–92; I. C. MacMillan and R. McGrath, "Discovering New Points of Differentiation," *Harvard Business Review*, July–August 1997, 133–145; I. C. MacMillan and R. G. McGrath, "Discover Your Products' Hidden Potential," *Harvard Business Review*, May–June 1996, 58–68; I. C. MacMillan, A. B. van Putten, R. G. McGrath, and J. D. Thompson, "Using Real Options Discipline for Highly Uncertain Technology Investments," *Research Technology Management* 49, no. 1 (2006): 29.

18. Macquarie Digital, "Brambles Limited: CEO Interview with Tom Gorman."

Chapter 6

1. "No Country Has a Company Like Ours," *El Pais*, June 17, 2007.

2. C. E. Brett, "Presentation of the Harrell L. Strimple Award of the Paleontological Society to Thomas E. Whiteley," and T. E. Whiteley, "Response," *Journal of Paleontology* 79, no. 4 (2005): 831–834.

3. S. N. Chakravarty and R. Simon, "Has the World Passed Kodak By?" *Forbes*, November 5, 1984.

4. S. W. Morten and M. W. Ellmann, *Yellow Journalism!* (New York: Wertheim & Co., 1984).

5. E. H. Bowman, "Strategy and the Weather," *Sloan Management Review*, Winter 1976, 49.

6. D. Daye and B. VanAuken, "Category First. Brand Second," Branding Strategy Insider, www.brandingstrategyinsider.com/2009/09/category-first-brand-second.html.

7. R. C. Alexander and D. K. Smith, *Fumbling the Future: How Xerox Invented, Then Ignored, the First Personal Computer* (New York: iUniverse, 1999).

8. W. Klepper, *The CEO's Boss: Tough Love in the Boardroom* (New York: Columbia Business School, 2010).

9. G. Sargut and R. G. McGrath, "Learning to Live with Complexity," *Harvard Business Review*, September 2011, 68–76.

10. E. Ries, *The Lean Startup: How Today's Entrepreneurs Use Continuous Innovation to Create Radically Successful Businesses* (New York: Crown Business, 2011).

11. R. G. McGrath and I. C. MacMillan, "Discovery-Driven Planning," *Harvard Business Review*, July 1995, 44–54; R. G. McGrath and I. C. MacMillan, *Discovery-Driven Growth: A Breakthrough Process to Reduce Risk and Seize Opportunity* (Boston: Harvard Business Press, 2009).

12. S. Key, "The Man—The Legend—John Osher, Inventor of the Spin Brush. Part II," AllBusiness, 2008, www.allbusiness.com/marketing-advertising/market-research-analysis/7665600-1.html#axzz2DXqrOvbZ.

13. M. A. Whiting and C. J. Bennett, *Driving Towards "0": Best Practices in Safety and Health*, Research Report R-1334-03-RR (New York: The Conference Board, 2004).

Chapter 7

1. S. Greenhouse, "A Part-Time Life as Hours Shrink and Shift," *New York Times*, October 27, 2012.

2. A. McGahan, *How Industries Evolve: Principles for Achieving and Sustaining Superior Performance* (Boston: Harvard Business School Press, 2004).

3. S. Tully, "*Fortune* 500: Profits Bounce Back," *Fortune*, May 3, 2010, 32.

4. AFL-CIO, "CEO Pay: Feeding the 1%," 2011, www.aflcio.org/corporatewatch/paywatch/paywatch2011_indexmore.cfm.

5. P. Gottschalk and S. Danziger, "Inequality in Wage Rates, Earnings and Family Income in the United States, 1975–2002," *Review of Income and Wealth* 51, no. 2 (2005): 231–254; M. Morris and B. Western, "Inequality in Earnings at the Close of the Twentieth Century," *Annual Review of Sociology* 25 (1999): 623–657.

6. J. Assa, "Inequality and Growth Re-Examined," *Technology and Investment* 3, no. 1 (2012): 1–6.

7. R. Safian, "This Is Generation Flux: Meet the Pioneers of the New (and Chaotic) Frontier of Business," *Fast Company*, January 9, 2012, 60–97.

8. F. R. Myers, *Get the Job You Want, Even When No One's Hiring: Take Charge of Your Career, Find a Job You Love, and Earn What You Deserve* (New York: John Wiley & Sons, 2009).

9. A. Horowitz, "15 People Who Were Fired Before They Became Filthy Rich," *Business Insider*, April 25, 2011, www.businessinsider.com/15-people-who-were-fired-before-they-became-filthy-rich-2011-4?op=1.

10. D. Wakabayashi and A. Troianovski, "Japan's Masayoshi Son Picks a Fight with U.S. Phone Giants," *Wall Street Journal*, November 24, 2012.

Index

About the Author

Rita Gunther McGrath, a professor at Columbia Business School, is a globally recognized expert on strategy in uncertain and volatile environments. Her thinking is highly regarded by readers and by clients that include Pearson, Coca-Cola Enterprises, General Electric, Alliance Boots, and the World Economic Forum. She is a popular instructor, a sought-after speaker, and a consultant to senior leadership teams. She was recognized as one of the top twenty management thinkers by global management award Thinkers50 in 2011. She's also been recognized as one of the top ten business school professors to follow on Twitter. In 2009, she was inducted as a fellow of the Strategic Management Society, an honor accorded those who have had a significant impact on the field. In 2013 she will serve as dean of the fellows.

McGrath has coauthored three previous books: *Discovery-Driven Growth: A Breakthrough Process to Reduce Risk and Seize Opportunity* (2009), *MarketBusters: 40 Strategic Moves That Drive Exceptional Business Growth* (2005), and *The Entrepreneurial Mindset* (2000), all published by Harvard Business Review Press. *MarketBusters* has been translated into ten languages and was named one of the best business books of 2005 by *strategy+business*. It was featured by Bill Gates at the 2005 Microsoft CEO Summit, whose theme, "New Pathways to Growth," was derived from the book's main topic.

McGrath has written many *Harvard Business Review* articles, including the best-selling "Discovery-Driven Planning" (1995), recognized now as an early articulation of today's "lean" start-up movement. She is also a highly respected researcher whose work has won awards from the most prestigious management journals.

McGrath appears regularly on television and radio and is often cited in the press, having been featured in the *Wall Street Journal*, *New York Times*, *Financial Times*, *BusinessWeek*, *Fast Company*, and *Inc.*, among others.

McGrath joined the faculty of Columbia Business School in 1993. Prior to life in academia, she was an information technology director, worked in the political arena, and founded two start-ups. She received her PhD from the Wharton School, University of Pennsylvania, and has degrees from Barnard College and the Columbia School of International and Public Affairs. She is married and is proud to be the mother of two delightful grownups.

For more information on McGrath, visit www.ritamcgrath.com or follow her on Twitter at @rgmcgrath.